Studies in the Begoniaceae

TABLE OF CONTENTS

STUDIES IN THE BEGONIACEAE

by

Andrey I Baranov

INTRODUCTORY NOTE

by

Dr Fred A Barkley

In the course of his excellent study on the morphology of *Begonia* inflorescences while working for his master's degree at Northeastern University, Mr Baranov became interested (as I had been for some time) in the botanical history of the genus *Begonia* Furthermore, during his research, it soon became obvious that our present knowledge of the floral morphology of many species was inadequate or almost lacking I am pleased to find that he has carried those interests to the production of this paper which should make a notable start toward supplying information in this area.

PREFACE

This work is a revised and updated version of the author's thesis submitted in 1973 at Northeastern University, Boston

The most important changes made in the course of preparation of this work were as follows:

1) the thesis title "A Comparative Study of the Gross Morphology of the Inflorescences and Flowers of *Begonia*" was changed to a new one: "Studies in the Begoniaceae",

2) the body of the paper was divided for topical reasons into two parts each of which is individually titled; thus, the first part is entitled "A Brief Taxonomic History of the Family Begoniaceae," while the second part is called "New Floral Information A Basis for Taxonomic Discussion of some Rare *Begonia* Species",

3) research related to the study of *Begonia* inflorescences was excluded from this work because *Begonia* inflorescences have been exhaustively studied by Irmscher in the early 1900's and there is very little that can be added to that study

The preparation of this paper was prompted by the need for more knowledge of both the taxonomic history of the group and of the floral morphology of the members of the genus *Begonia* As a material for the study, the flowers of the species currently available in greenhouses in the Boston area have been used When selecting these species, all garden varieties and hybrids were excluded and twenty-three species noteworthy for their rareness were studied. Most of those species are from the Neotropical region (Brazil 10, Mexico 3, the Americas 1, Argentina 1, Bolivia 1, Colombia 1) and the remainder from the Paleotropical region (India 2, Indo-China 1, Sumatra 2, Tropical Africa 1) * All these plants occur in wild condition in the aforementioned regions.

Taxonomically these species belong to sixteen sections, out of eighty-one** currently known in the genus *Begonia* Among these sections are such large and important groups as Begonia, Huszia, Petermannia, Pritzelia, and Reichenheimia. Expecially interesting among these is the section Pritzelia, the numerous members of which exhibit much variation in their structure. It is hoped that flower structures typical of the various members of the genus *Begonia* are

*The count is made according to F A Barkley, [4].

**According to Baranov, A and Barkley, F.A., [2].

represented adequately The members of the genus *Begonia* described in this work are illustrated with a number of drawings arranged in twenty-three plates and four separate figures

The completion of this work to a large extent depended on the support and assistance of many people The invaluable help with the organization and preparation of the manuscript, as well as encouragement and support of Prof F.A. Barkley are herewith gratefully acknowledged I should also like to thank the administration of the Northeastern University Greenhouses (Woburn, Massachusetts) and Mr Michael Kartuz, of the Kartuz Greenhouses (Wilmington, Massachusetts) for their willingness to supply *Begonia* flower material for this study Furthermore, my gratitude is extended to the Gray and Arnold Arboretum libraries and to the library of the Royal Botanical Gardens, Kew, England, for supplying copies of scarce publications and photographs of rare illustrations Finally, I should like to thank my daughter, Elena Baranov, for her suggestions and assistance

A BRIEF TAXONOMIC HISTORY OF THE FAMILY BEGONIACEAE

Botanical descriptions of plant species published before 1753 are considered not official because 1753, the year of publication of Linnaeus' "Species Plantarum," marks the beginning of modern botanical nomenclature According to Barkley [3], the first nine species of *Begonia* were discovered and described before 1753. These were from both Neotropical and Paleotropical regions, they were described under various names, and only in post-Linnaean time were they re-classified and re-named as *Begonia* species The list of these species is given in Table I

The species in the table are arranged in chronological order of the dates of their description. The earliest one described, in this series of species, is *Totoncaxoxo coyollin* (Fig 1) Its description was published in 1651. However, there are indications that this plant was discovered as early as 1577 [35]. There are, likewise, differences between the date of discovery and the date of publication of other species in the series Thus, Rumpf discovered the plant he called *Empetrum acetosum* in 1654, but published its description in 1747 [31], Sloan discovered his *Aceris fructu herba anomala . .* in 1688 and published its description in 1696 [32], and Plumier found his species of in 1690 and his finding was published in 1700 by Tournefort [36]

The credit for the discovery of the plant which first was given the name *Begonia* is usually given to Charles Plumier In 1690, this Franciscan monk and early botanist, had found a plant in the West Indies that had no clear relationship with any of the known genera of plants Consequently, a new genus was proposed by Plumier (1703) who named it in honor of Michel Begon, French Superintendent of Santo Domingo (1638-1710), who was Plumier's patron and an amateur botanist The incomplete herbarium specimens of that plant reached Europe and were sufficient to describe the genus J P de Tournefort published Plumier's name and description in 1700 [36], three years before the appearance of Plumier's book [29] Tournefort's description reads as follows·

> Begonia est plantae genus, auctore Clariss. Plumerio, flore gemino, alio scilicet sterili A, ex quatuor petalis amplioribus B et angustioribus C composito; alio vero rosaceo D ex plurimis petalis E in orbem positis constante et calyci foliatio F insidentibus, is autem deinde abit in fructum G trigonum, alatum H, in tria loculamenta I divisum, seminibusque foetum exiguis L. Begoniae species sunt, . etc.*

---

*Translations of this description into English are not readily available and therefore one is offered:

> Begonia is a genus of plants, the author of which is the celebrated Plumier, with paired flowers, one [of them] is evidently sterile A and composed of four petals of which some are larger [broader] B and the others are narrower C,

TABLE I. A list of *Begonia* species described before 1753 with their Pre-Linnaean Synonymy.

No.	Post-Linnaean *Begonia* name	Author and Year	Pre-Linnaean Name	Author and Year	Species Native Origin	References
1.	*B. gracilis*	HBK 1825	*Totoncaxoxo coyollin*	Hernandez 1651	Mexico	[3, 15]
2.	*B. tuberosa*	Lamarck 1783	*Empetrum acetosum*	Rumpf 1747	East Indies	[3,31]
3.	*B. acutifolia*	Jacquin 1786	*Aceris fructu herba anomala . . .*	Sloane 1696	Jamaica	[3,32]
4.	*B. malabarica*	Lamarck 1783	*Tsjeria-narinampuli*	Rheede 1689	South India	[3,30]
			Acetosum Nigritarum	Camello 1704	Philippines	[3,9]
5.	*B. macrophylla*	Dryander 1791	*Begonia nivea . . .* *Begonia purpurea . . .* *Begonia roseo flore . . .*	Plumier 1703	West Indies	[3, 29]
6.	*B. nitida*	Dryander 1789	*Begonia roseo flore, folio . . . minor & glabro*	Plumier 1703	West Indies	[3, 29]
7.	*B. rotundifolia*	Lamarck 1783	*Begonia roseo flore, folio . . . minor & hirsuto*	Plumier 1703	West Indies	[3, 29]
8.	*B. grandis*	Dryander 1791	*Kaido Sjukaido*	Kaempfer 1712	Japan	[3, 19]
9.	*B. hirsuta*	Aublet 1775	*Begonia hirsuta, flore albo . . .*	Barrere 1741	South America	[3, 5]

The capital letters in the text of the description refer to the figures on Tournefort's plate (Fig. 3) and after the words: "The species of Begonia are . . " follows a list of six species of plants described by Plumier The names of the species are phrase-names (polynomials) as had been customary with the early botanists, e g *Begonia purpurea, maxima, folio aurito* Plumier.

According to Klotzsch [20], Plumier furnished his six species of *Begonia* with only fragmentary illustrations and described them very briefly so that these descriptions are entirely inadequate to provide a clear idea as to the characters of the genus and species. For this reason, continues Klotzsch, one has to make allowances for Linnaeus, who only had these incomplete descriptions available and lacked the opportunity to examine either the herbaria or live specimens of *Begonia* and therefore his treatment of the group contains inaccuracies.

The earliest description of the genus *Begonia* was made by Linnaeus in 1737 in the first edition of his "Genera Plantarum" [23]. On page 360 of this publication the genus is placed in the section "Fragmenta Tournefortiana" and its description is made in the following formal manner

Begonia Tournef. 442. vide H.M. IX 86 901
Masculus flos
Cal nullus· nisi corollam dicas
Cor. tetrapetala, patens, regularis. Petala duo opposita lanceolata· duo reliqua ovata, emarginata, latiora
Stam. Filamenta numerosa, corolla breviora, capillaria
Antherae subrotundae
Pist. caducum
*Hermaphroditus flos in eadem planta cum Masculis
Cal nullus, cujus vices gerit Germen
Cor Petala quinque, verticaliter cordata, oblonga, patentia
Stam. Filamenta numerosa, corolla breviora, capillaria.
Antherae subrotundae
Pist Germen sub receptaculo triangulare, angulis membranaceis, tricuspe, erectum. Styli tres, bifidi, longitudine staminum
Stigmata globosa
Per. triangulare, triloculare: tribus alis longitudinalibus.
Sem. numerosa, parva.
Obs. De numero staminum, de pericarpii specie (H M baccas commemorat) de pistillo masculi floris, nil certi scimus *

---

another flower is certainly rose-like D consisting of very numerous petals E always arranged in a circle [ring-like fashion] and with sitting on its outermost covering, on the other hand, is thereafter changing into fruit G having three angles and wings H, and divided into three chambers I with numerous seeds L. The species of Begonia are, . . . etc

*So far as is known to this writer this description has never before been translated into English Consequently, such a translation is offered below:

Figs. 1 - 4. Photographic copies of illustrations from historical books, exemplifying different stages in the study of the genus *Begonia*.

Figs. 1 - 3. The early period.

Fig. 4. The early modern period.

Fig. 1. *Totoncaxoxo coyollin*. From: Francisco Hernandez Medico. Nova Plantarum, Animalium et Mineralium Mexicanorum Historia. Rome. 1651. p. 195.

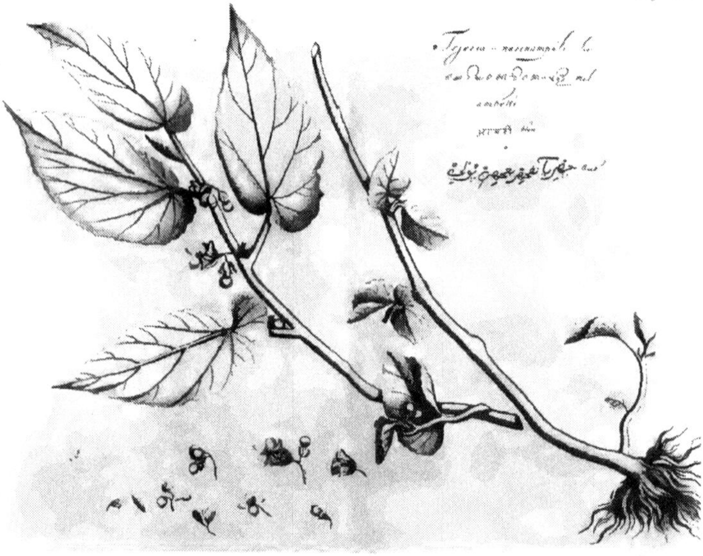

Fig. 2. *Tsjeria-narinampuli*. From: Van Rheede tot Drakestein, Henry Adrian. <u>Horti Malabarici pars nona, de Herbis</u> . . . .

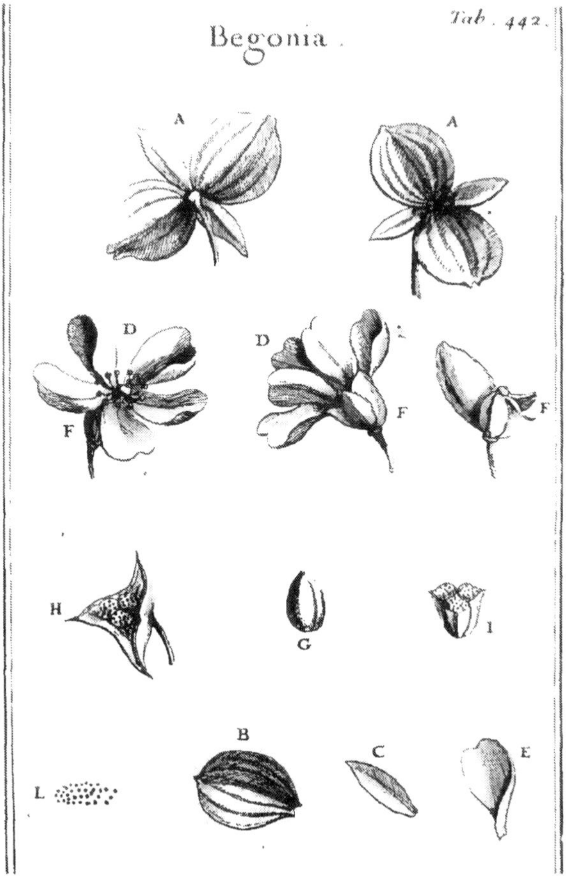

Fig. 3. *Begonia.* From: Tournefort, Joseph Pitton de. Institutiones Rei Herbariae . . . . Paris. 1700. Plate 442. This is the first illustration representing the flowering and fruiting structures of *Begonia.*

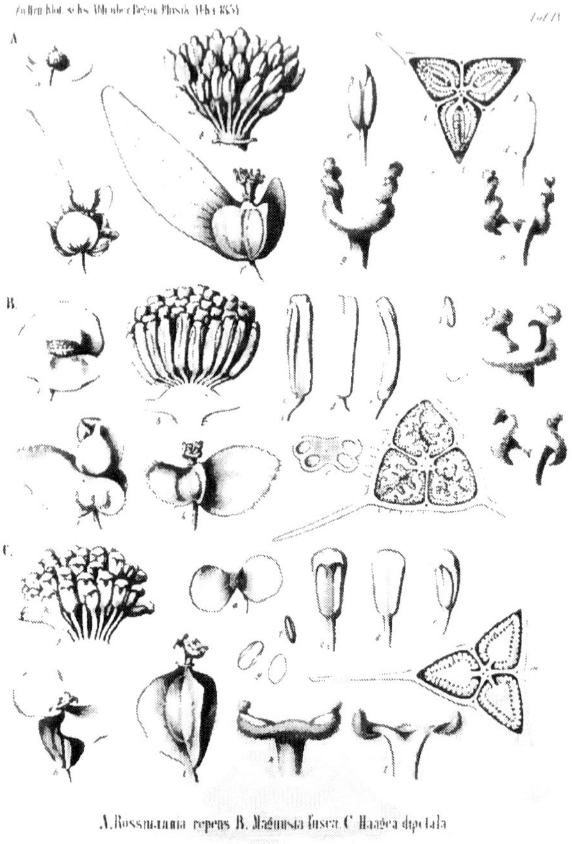

Fig. 4. A. *Rossmannia repens*; B. *Magnusia fusca*; C. *Haagea dipetala*. From: Klotzsch, J.F. Begoniaceen, Gatungen und Arten. Berlin. 1855. Plate IX.

Linnaean references in the above description are, first, to Tournefort ("Tournef 442") (for this reason the authority for the genus *Begonia* may be written *Begonia* [Tourn] L), and second, to van Rheede's work [30] ("H M IX 86") (Fig. 2) The Linnaean note at the end of the description explains why Linnaeus at that time did not know how to classify *Begonia* and therefore considered it as a "genus incertae sedis "

Aside from Tournefort and Linnaeus, description of the genus *Begonia* was offered in 1747 by C G. Ludwig under number 1044 on page 313 of his work [25] This description follows·

> Fragmenta varia
> 1044 BEGONIA Tourn Flos duplex in simplici planta
> Stamineus Calix nullus, corolla tetrapetala, duobus petalis latioribus, duobus angustioribus, stamina multa
> Perfectus Calix ovarium cingens, tricuspidatus, corolla rosacea, stamina multa, styli tres, bifidi, capsula triangularis; semina exigua.*

> Staminate flower
> Calyx none, if one does not mean by this term the corolla (Linnaeus and other early botanists understood under the term "calyx" different covering structures including the calyx proper).
> Corolla· of four petals, spreading, regular. Petals two opposite, lanceolate; two remaining are broader, ovate, emarginate
> Stamens filaments numerous, shorter than the corolla, hair-like
> Anthers almost round in outline
> Pistil· caducous
> Bisexual flower on the same plant with the staminate flowers
> Calyx lacking, instead of which the flower has the ovary
> Corolla Petals five, vertically cordate, oblong, spreading
> Stamens. filaments numerous, shorter than the corolla, hair-like
> Anthers almost round in outline.
> Pistil ovary erect with three cusps and is sitting under the receptacle and has three angles which are membranous Styles three, two-divided, of equal length with the stamens. Stigmata globose
> Fruit. triangular, with three chambers and three longitudinal wings
> Seeds numerous, small
> Note with respect to the number of stamens, type of fruit (according to H M. they resemble berries), and pistil in the staminate flowers we have no positive knowledge)

*This may be translated as follows·

> Various fragments
> 1044 *Begonia* Tourn Flowers of two kinds on one and the same plant
> Staminate [flower]. Calyx none, corolla of four petals, with two broader and two more narrow petals, stamens numerous
> Perfect [hermaphrodite] [flower]. Calyx encircling ovary, with three cusps; corolla like a flower of a single rose, stamens numerous,

Six years after Ludwig, Linnaeus published his "Species Plantarum" [24], the work from which modern botanical nomenclature took its beginning. In this publication, *Begonia* is placed under the class Polygamia dioecia on page 1056 In the description, Linnaeus included under the name *Begonia obliqua*, all species previously noted by Plumier, Sloane and Barrere, thus making the identify of the species quite unclear [3].

Eventually Lamarck [21] and Jacquin [18] attempted to correct Linnaeus' error and revalidate the originally described species, but neither one of them was able to examine more than one species. Furthermore, to distinguish a species from other species, these authors give very scanty information borrowed from the literature and as a result, their attempt proved to be unsuccessful.

Thus, the first botanist to provide a really clear description of the genus *Begonia* was Dryander [13] On November 3, 1789, he read a paper entitled "Observations upon the genus *Begonia*" at the Linnaean Society. In this presentation, he distinguished twenty-one species of *Begonia*, of these, eleven species were from South America, seven from the East Indies and three from the islands off the eastern coast of Africa. He had an opportunity to examine three live species from the West Indies because since 1777, living *Begonia* were brought to Europe and in the 1780's Kew possessed five species. For this reason, Dryander could improve on the circumscriptions of the genus and the species, and provide better definitions of their characters than had been possible for his predecessors. Additional credit must be given to Dryander for directing his attention to *Begonia* foliage-leaf characters and for utilizing them for taxonomic purposes.

In the subsequent period of European exploration and expansion overseas, the knowledge about exotic plants, including *Begonia*, was substantially increased. Thus, through publication of descriptions of live specimens of *Begonia*, imported into Europe, as well as those of botanical materials collected by the explorers in South America, East Indies and the Cape of Good Hope, genus *Begonia* already included many species by the beginning of the nineteenth century Approximately at that time, namely in the second decade of the nineteenth century, several leading European botanists proposed to consider this group as a family or as a "natural order" as it had been called in the botanical language of that period.

Before the introduction of the principles of uniformity and stability into the botanical nomenclature, the credit for the establishment of the family Begoniaceae had been given to various people Thus, Klotzsch [20], Lindley [22], Endlicher [14], and Bentham and Hooker *f* [6] give first credit to Robert Brown [8], A. De Candolle [11] to Aime Bonpland [7]; Pfeiffer [28]

---

styles three, two-divided, capsule triangular,
seed little.

All three descriptions of the genus *Begonia* mentioned above are not official from the point of view of modern botanical nomenclature, and are inaccurate from a botanical viewpoint to Klotzsch, and Index Kewensis [16] to Bentham and Hooker f. But when the rules of botanical nomenclature became accepted and the starting points for the names of taxa in the Spermatophyta became approved, this practice became inconsistent with the rules of nomenclature For this reason and because the proposals by Brown and Bonpland were informal, the credit for the establishment of the family Begoniaceae has been given to C.A. Agardh and the familial name "Begoniaceae" proposed by him has been retained against all other names for future use [34]

Agardh [1] provided the first formal description of the family Begoniaceae indicating that the essential characters of this new taxon are diclinous or bisexual flowers, without a corolla; three to many stamens, three styles, and triangulate, polyspermous capsules Agardh included two genera into the family Begoniaceae. *Begonia* L with 35 species and *Houttuynia* Th with one species In an accompanying note, Agardh described how *Begonia* was classified by his predecessors -- Linnaeus, Sprengel, Batsch and Adanson, and especially Bonpland who was the first to advance the idea of the separation of *Begonia* into a family by itself.

By the 1850's, the number of species in the genus *Begonia* increased to more than two hundred, and then, in 1855, J.F Klotzsch published his revision of the group (which he treated as a family) under the title of "Begoniaceen--Gattungen und Arten" [20]. Klotzsch studied the abundant material in the Royal Herbarium at Berlin, which contained collections by Ruiz, A. von Humboldt and Moritz, from the different parts of South America, and specimens gathered by Warsczevicz from Central America, and Sello from Brazil, he also had access to a hundred species of live *Begonia* in the botanical garden at Schoneberg. In his work, he supplied descriptions and beautiful illustrations (Fig. 4) of flower studies of about 170 species which he grouped into 41 genera. At this point, it is relevant to note that Klotzsch's work represents a landmark in the history of the study of *Begonia* because it marks the starting point for a modern approach to the treatment of the group Klotzsch's studies of the gross morphology of *Begonia* flowers considerably improved the knowledge of these structures and offered possibilities for the utilization of flower characters in *Begonia* classification Klotzsch, according to C.B Clarke [10], had based his classification of *Begonia* on the differences in the shape of the styles with complicated stigmas and on the stamen morphology which he considered as taxonomic characters of primary significance The classification of the Begoniaceae developed by Klotzsch, did not survive in its original form, but it did provide the basis for the classifications advanced by De Candolle and subsequent authors Thus, Klotzsch's survey of *Begonia* represented an entirely different approach from all the previous investigations of this genus.

In the post-Klotzschian period, although some scholars made minor contributions to the study of the begonias, Klotzsch's work found worthy successors first, in De Candolle and second, in C.B. Clarke. In the latter part of the nineteenth century, De Candolle not only described a number of sections and many species new to science, but he also reworked Klotzsch's classification of the group in such a way that it is still the basis of modern concepts of the genus The new classification was presented in the fifteenth volume of De Candolle's "Prodromus Systematis Regni Vegetabilis" [11]

De Candolle reduced Klotzsch's 41 genera down to three, namely *Casparya* *Begonia* and *Mezierea*, which he differentiated from each other on the basis of the fruit structure and the mode of fruit dehiscence All other genera he reduced to the rank of sections adding to them a number of new sections so that their total number in his classification was 69 The distribution of sections among the genera is as follows 1) eight sections with 23 species in *Casparya*, 2) 59 sections including 398 species and cultivars divided into three series with 1, 21 and 37 sections, respectively in *Begonia*, and 3) 2 sections with three species in *Mezierea*. Thus, the total number of species and cultivars became 424, or had more than doubled since Klotzsch's work, due largely to the discovery of new species

C B Clarke [10], developed his own system of classification of the genus *Begonia* in which he grouped the members of the genus into six subgenera. (1) Casparya, (2) Parvibegonia, (3) Alaecida, (4) Aschisma, (5) Eu-Begonia, and (6) Platycentrum These subgenera were established on the basis of the number of cells in the fruit and the mode of the fruit dehiscence. In naming his subgenera, Clarke utilized the terms which were previously brought into use partly by Klotzsch and partly by de Candolle

De Candolle's system of classification of the Begoniaceae remained essentially unchanged until 1895, when O Warburg published his revision of the family Begoniaceae [37]. Warburg's infrageneric classification of the genus *Begonia* was basically a modification of De Candolle and C.B Clarke's systems whereby Warburg retained only one genus, *Begonia* All of the taxa considered by Klotzsch, De Candolle and Clarke as genera or as subgenera were treated as sections. He reduced the number of old sections and incorporated new sections and species so that in the final product the number of sections was 62 and the number of species about 470 In addition, the sections in the Warburg's classification were divided into four geographical groups (1) African, (2) Asiatic, (3) American, and (4) American-Asiatic sections, as well as two groups, with one section each, of indefinite systematic position

Like De Candolle's approach, Warburg's classification lasted for about thirty years and was superseded in 1925 by E. Irmscher's study which was included in the second edition of the "Pflanzenfamilien" [17]. In general, Irmscher followed Warburg's classification of the group and the changes that he made in that system were rather insignificant. For example, in the diagnoses of sections Irmscher, with unfailing regularity, mentions the number of locules in the ovary, while Warburg is not that punctilious in this respect. In regard to the taxonomic treatment, Irmscher's classification of *Begonia* is a duplication of that by Warburg, although he did include in it two new sections (Apteron C DC. and Warburgina O. Kuntze) and did list a considerably larger number of species. Irmscher's work has been the last general survey of the Begoniaceae and since its publication no other account of this nature has been published. But the sections and species of *Begonia* have been and are still being studied by a number of botanists. These scholars argue that some sections contain very diverse members and probably should be divided, at the same time some recent studies indicate that a few should be united This taxonomic revision debate is very important because it can lead to the establishment of an evolutionary classification

The genus *Begonia* is the type genus of the family and the largest group of species within this family with approximately eighty sections and over a thousand species according to the latest studies, of which 144 species are not assigned to any section [2], [4] For this reason it seems logical that, so far, the discussion has been focused on this genus. Aside from the aforementioned genus, several others are usually included in the family, although their number varies among different authors Warburg, for example [37] puts forth four genera *Hillebrandia, Begonia, Symbegonia* and *Begoniella*; Irmscher [17] recognizes five genera in the family, namely all those suggested by Warburg plus genus *Semibegoniella* Modern botanists, especially in the United States, usually acknowledge only three genera *Hillebrandia, Symbegonia* and *Begonia*.

Of these genera, genus *Hillebrandia* described by Oliver [26] has the following requisite characters perianth of ten parts in two cycles both in the pistillate and staminate flowers, with the inner parts very small, ovary not completely inferior, fruit indehiscent, but with carpels gaping between the styles in the upper part, placentation parietal

Genus *Symbegonia* established by Warburg [37] has the following characters perianth parts are less than ten, and are in one cycle, in staminate flowers the perianth parts are two and free, while in the pistillate flowers the perianth is of united parts, stamens are numerous, with the rest of the characters similar to those of *Begonia*.

Genera *Semibegoniella* and *Begoniella* were described by de Candolle [12] and by Oliver [28] respectively The characters of *Semibegoniella* are staminate perianth gamotepalous, with three to five lobes on the apex, pistillate perianth of six free parts, stamens eight, arising on a column, ovary inferior, three-celled, horned, placentae undivided. The characters of *Begoniella* are: staminate perianth gamotepalous, with four lobes; stamens four, arising on a short column; pistillate perianth gamopetepalous, with four lobes, ovary inferior, three-celled, three-winged; placentae undivided.

In a revision of the South American species of *Begonia*, Smith and Schubert [33] argue that the characters by which *Semibegoniella* and *Begoniella* are differentiated, are insufficient as generic characters, and that both of these are consectional with the section Casparya of *Begonia* Consequently, all species of *Begoniella* and *Semibegoniella* must be combined with section Casparya This is the reason why modern American specialists of the Begoniaceae do not recognize the validity of the genera *Begoniella* and *Semibegoniella*.

References Cited

1. Agardh, C.A. 1825. Aphorismi Botanici. Lund. p. 200.

2. Baranov, A. & Barkley, F.A. 1974. The Sections of the Genus Begonia. Northeastern University, Boston. 28 pp.

3. Barkley, Fred A. 1968. Begoniaceae to 1763. Providence. 22 pp.

4. ______________. 1972. The Species of the Begoniaceae: The Genera, sections and known species of each. Buxtonian **1**: Suppl. 5.

5. Barrere, Pierre. 1741. Essai sur l'Histoire Naturelle de la France Equinoxiale, ou de 'Nembrement Des Plantes, des Animaux, & des Mineraux, que . . . avec leurs noms differens . . . & quelques Observations sur leur usage dans la Medicine & dans les Artes. Paris. pp. 21-22.

6. Bentham, G. & Hooker, J.D. 1865-1867. Genera Plantarum 1. London. p. 841.

7. Bonpland, Aimé 1817. Description des plantes rares cultivees a Malmaison et a Navarre. Part 11: 153-157. Paris.

8. Brown, Robert. 1818. Observations, Systematical and Geographical . . . Appendix V in: J.K. Tucky R.N. Narrative of an Expedition to Explore the River Zaire . . . . London. p. 464.

9. Camello, Georgius Josephus, S.J. 1704. Herbarium aliarumque Stirpium in Insula Luzone et Philippinarum. Appendix to Jeannis Raii Historiae Plantarum, tomus tertius . . . . p. 14.

10. Clarke, C.B. 1881. On Indian Begonias. Jour. Linn. Soc. Bot. London **18**: 114-122.

11. De Candolle, Alphonse. 1864. Begoniaceae. Prodromus Systematis Naturalis Regni Vegetabilis. **15**, 1: 266-408. 517.

12. De Candolle, Casimir. 1908. *Semibegoniella* C.DC. n. gen. Bull. de l'Herbier Boiss. 2 ser, **8** (5): 327-328.

13. Dryander, Jonas. 1791. Observations on the genus of *Begonia*. Trans. Linn. Soc. London. Vol. I: 155-173.

14. Endlicher, S. 1836-1840. Genera Plantarum. Vienna. p. 941.

15. Hernandez Medico, Francisco. 1651. Nova Plantarum, Animalium et Mineralium Mexicanorum Historia. Rome.

16 Index Kewensis. 1893 Fasc I Oxford p 283

17 Irmscher, E. 1925 Begoniaceae Engler u Prantl, Die Naturlichen Pflanzenfamilien (Ed 2) **21** 548-588

18 Jacquin, Nicolas Joseph 1786 Collectanea ad Botanicam . .

19 Kaempfer, Engelbert 1712 Amoenitatum Exoticarum Politico Physico-Medicarum . quibut continentur Observationes & Descriptiones vol 5 Lemgo p 888.

20 Klotzsch, J.F 1855 Begoniaceen, Gattungen und Arten. Berlin

21 Lamarck, J.P.B.A. Monet Chevalier de 1785 Encyclopedie Methodique, Botanique **1** 392-394

22 Lindley, John 1836. A Natural System ed 2 London p 56

23 Linnaeus, Carolus. 1737. Genera Plantarum Eorumque Characteres naturales Secundum Leiden p 360.

24 ____________ 1753 Species Plantarum, exhibentes Plantas Rite Cognitas, ad Genera Relatas, . . Secundum Systema Sexuale Digestas vol. 2. Stockholm p 1056

25 Ludwig, Christian Gottlieb 1747. Definitiones Generum Plantarum . . . Lippstadt, p 313.

26 Oliver, Daniel 1866 On *Hillebrandia* A new Genus of the Begoniaceae. Trans Linn. Soc London **25** (3)· 361-363, 1 pl.

27. ____________. 1873 On *Begoniella*, A new Genus of Begnoiaceae from New Grenada Trans. Linn. Soc. London. **28** (4). 513-514 1 pl

28. Pfeiffer, L 1873 Nomenclator Botanicus. I (1). Cassel. p 384

29 Plumier, Charles 1703. Catalogus Plantarum Americanum. Paris.

30 Rheede tot Drakestein, Henry Adrian van. 1689. Horti Malabarici, pars nona, de Herbis . . Amsterdam

31 Rumpf, Georg Everhard. 1747 Herbarium Amboinense, Plurimas complectans arbores, . Amsterdam.

32 Sloane, Hans 1696 Catalogus Plantarum Quae in Insula Jamaca sponte proveniunt, . . . London.

33. Smith, L B & B G Schubert. 1955. Studies in the Begoniaceae. *Jour Wash Acad. Sci.* **45**(4): 110-114.

34. Stafleu, F A (Ed.). 1972 Nomina Familiarum Conservanda *Intern. Code of Bot Nomenclature* Appendix II Utrecht p 224.

35. Thompson, Mildred L. 1976. A Brief History of the Begoniaceae *Thompson Begonia Guide* ed 2, **1**, Introduction, pp XI-XVI

36 Tournefort, Joseph Pitton de 1700 *Institutiones Rei Herbariae* . . Paris

37. Warburg, Otto. 1895 Begoniaceae Engler u Prantl. *Die naturlichen Pflanzenfamilien* **3**, 6a 121-150.

NEW FLORAL INFORMATION. A BASIS FOR TAXONOMIC DISCUSSION OF SOME RARE BEGONIA SPECIES

Materials and Methods

Fresh *Begonia* flowers were collected in the Northeastern University Greenhouses (Woburn, Massachusetts) and in the Kartuz Greenhouses (Wilmington, Massachusetts) and fixed in 70% alcohol The finding of both staminate and pistillate flowers for this study has been connected with great difficulties and has eliminated a number of species which the writer would have liked to include in this work The fixed material subsequently has been dissected and studied in the laboratory with the help of a Bausch and Lomb Stereo Microscope with 10 X wide field eyepieces and magnifications of 7.5 X, 15 X, 25 X and 60 X. The parts of the flowers have been measured, briefly described and drawn. Twenty-three species have been studied by this method and this resulted in about 276 drawings which are arranged on twenty-three plates.

The illustrations and descriptions of the *Begonia* flowers have been made with the purpose of demonstrating structural differences among various species and sections of *Begonia* The descriptions of sections and species have been taken from literature and, when it was necessary, translated into English

Begonia Flowers

The flowers in begonias are asymmetrical, monoecious, heterochlamydeous There is no real distinction, however, between calyx and corolla, and therefore the perianth parts are called tepals They are petaloid and usually colored white, pink, red or less often yellow, but never blue.

The tepals of the staminate flowers are usually either two or four, but in general their number varies over wider limits, very seldom more than ten (5 + 5),* most often they are two to four (2 + 0 or 2 + 2), less often eight (2 + 6). The tepals are usually free, and the two inner ones are usually smaller or narrower than the others. When the tepals are four, they are usually arranged oppositely cross-wise Stamens are numerous and are arranged in many cycles Filaments are free or in many species they are more or less united below. The short filaments often arise on the tip of a cylindrical column, or filaments may arise on all sides and on different levels along the column, or they may arise on only one side of the column. Completely united filaments are very rare and possibly are not to be found in *Begonia*. Anthers are basifixed and always free, but are of different shapes. They are usually ovate or oblong, less often rounded (orbicular) or linear, dehiscing in most cases by long or short lateral slits, however, in some species they dehisce by

*A large number of tepals is typically produced in several cultivars of *Begonia*.

terminal pores The connective is often more or less protracted and may overhang. It is mostly broadly blunt, seldom narrow and filamentous (filiform). The rudiments of ovary, under normal conditions, are completely absent from the staminate flower.

The tepals of the pistillate flowers are two or five (seldom six or nine), free, usually unequal (the inner ones are smaller), often persistent. The styles are two to six, often somewhat united below, usually two- to four-parted, seldom with a larger number of branches. Style branches are straight or often twisted, usually awl-shaped, seldom thick and short Stigmatic surfaces are usually band-shaped, covering stigmatic branches in a helical fashion with one, two, or three twists For the most part the stigmatic surface is continuous on both branches of the style, seldom at the base of the style it has an interrupted-helical portion. In a few species the style branches are evenly covered on all sides with stigmatic papillae or a stigmatic tissue covers the capitate, crescent-shaped or reniform ends of the stigmatic branches. The ovary is inferior, usually three-celled, less often two-celled, and as an exception four- to six-celled, usually furnished with one to three ribs, horns or wings. The placentae are inserted in the inner corners of the cells and seldom on the lateral walls of the ovary, they are usually two-parted, seldom with larger number of lobes. Rarely in one and the same ovary the split and non-split placentae might be found Ovules are numerous, anatropous or rarely orthotropous

Previous authors did not pay much attention to the structure of the stigmatic papillae In the course of this study the structure of the stigmatic surfaces of each species studied has been carefully checked, and significant differences have been noted under the discussion of each species * And finally, flower disposition in *Begonia* are in inflorescences that are either terminal or axillary

Descriptions of Begonia Species

Below are given the descriptions of twenty-three species of *Begonia* which have been studied for this paper The descriptions of the species are given under the sections to which they belong and the sections included in this study are arranged in alphabetical order. The descriptions given are translated from various publications by authors such as Alphonse De Candolle [6], Warburg [9] and Irmscher [8], the names of the type species of the sections are given according to "The Sections of the Genus *Begonia*" by Barkley and Baranov (1974) [3] Modifications and additions to the existing descriptions from the literature have been made whenever additional information has been found. The accompanying illustrations are original.

---

*A more detailed report on the study of stigmatic surfaces in the Begoniaceae was published by this author [4], [5].

Section BARYA (Klotzsch) A DC , Ann.Sci Nat Bot. 4,11. 122 1859

Staminate flower· Tepals four, these are erect, narrow, lanceolate, filaments arising on all sides of a very elongated, slender column, anthers ovate, approximately of an equal length with the filaments, connective obtuse, overhanging

Pistillate flower tepals four to six, erect, acute, lanceolate, styles three, united a little below, persistent, with long, erect branches that continue to grow, stigmatic papillae make up a continuous helical band with five turns, placentae divided (split) Fruit three-celled with one large and two small wings.

Semi-shrubs with palmately or palmate-pinnately veined leaves Inflorescence few-flowered, axillary Mostly Bolivia and Peru

Type species. *Begonia monadelpha* Klotzsch
Species examined: *Begonia boliviensis* A DC.

Begonia boliviensis A. DC , Ann Sci Nat Bot ser 4, 11 122 1859 (Plate I)

Glabrous, leaves narrow, lanceolate, acuminate, pinnately-palmately veined; broadly rounded at the base, margin serrate-dentate; stipules lanceolate, inflorescence few-flowered, tepals of the pistillate flowers five to six, long and narrowly lanceolate

Staminate flower: pedicel 0 83 cm long, tepals four, at right angles with each other, 2.8 - 3.1 cm long, 1 cm broad, inner tepals 2 8 cm long, 0 3 cm broad, androecium 1.25 cm long, 0 4 cm broad; stamens 0 35 cm long, anther 0 15 cm long, filaments 0.2 cm long, the connective in specimens studied were not overhanging

Pistillate flower pedicels 1 7 cm long, tepals five, 2 1 - 2 4 cm long, 0.3 - 0 45 cm broad, styles three, twice divided, with very long branches, stigmatic surface forms helical bands, stigmatic papillae of pinnacle-like type; ovary three-celled, 0 7 cm long, 0 2 cm broad, with three unequal wings, the largest wing 0.8 cm broad, the smaller wings 0.15 - 0.2 cm broad, placentae two-parted

Section BEGONIA (Baranov & Barkley), Phytologia 24.155. 1972

Staminate flower tepals four (rarely two), filaments mostly free, less often united below; anthers oblong, obtuse, as long as or a little longer than the filaments; connective very little overhanging.

Pistillate flower tepals five to six (usually five), styles three, persistent or falling off, shortly united below, two-parted, often with twisted branches, stigmatic surface continuous, helically band-shaped; placentae two-parted, fruit three-celled, with three unequal wings.

Mostly erect (seldom subscandent) herbs or semishrubs, sometimes with tuberous bases and small bulbils in the leaf axils, leaves palmately-pinnately veined or pinnately veined (rarely palmately veined), mostly oblique and acute; cystoliths none

Type species *Begonia acutifolia* Jacquin
Species examined: *Begonia cucullata* Willd var *hookeri*, Smith and Schubert, *B pseudo-lubbersii* Brade, *B. schmidtiana* Regl.

Begonia cucullata Willd , Sp Pl 4·414
1805, v *hookeri* Smith & Schubert, Darwiniana
5·104 1941. (Plate II)

Caulescent plant, leaves obliquely cordate, serrulate, widely ovate, subtruncate at base, petioles short, stipules oblong, dentate, large.

Staminate flower pedicel 0.7 cm long, tepals four, to 18 mm long, the two outer opposite ones larger, the inner pair smaller and narrower, incumbent, external tepals oblong-orbiculate, 0 9 cm long, 0 9 cm broad, internal tepals spatulate, 0 6 cm long, 0 3 cm broad, androecium ca 0.5 cm long, ca 0.7 cm broad, stamens of two kinds, outer stamens short-filamented (anthers 0 25 cm long, filaments 0 14 cm long) and inner ones long-filamented (anthers 0 25 cm long, filaments 0 23 cm long), connective dilated towards apex, strongly overhanging.

Pistillate flower· pedicel 0 9 cm long, with four bracteoles (two of these are near the base of the pedicel, two others at the base of the ovary), tepals five, 0 7 - 1 0 cm long, 0.4 - 0 6 cm broad; styles three, two-divided, branches ca. 0 4 cm long, twisted, evenly covered with stigmatic surface, stigmatic papillae form conical, pyramid-like piles, ovary three-celled, 1.1 cm long, 0.5 cm broad, with three subequal wings (0.5, 0.48 and 0 38 cm long); placentae divided into two narrow lobes, seeds strongly obtuse

Begonia pseudo-lubbersii Brade, Arquiv. Jard Bot.
Rio de Janeiro 15.36, t.5. 1957 (Plate III)

Medium-sized, glabrous semi-shrub; stems 0.6 - 0 8 m tall, erect, 0 3 - 0 5 cm in diameter; leaves membranous, glabrous, obliquely lanceolate-oblong, obliquely cordate at the base, indistinctly remotely denticulate at the margin, 8 - 12 cm long, 3 - 4 cm broad, petioles slender, glabrous, 2.5 - 5.5 cm long; stipules persistent, broadly ovate or oblong, entire, glabrous; inflorescence cymous, few-flowered.

Staminate flower pedicel 0.6 cm long, tepals four cross-wise oppositely arranged, external tepals 2 5 cm long, 2 3 cm broad, very broad ovate-orbiculate,

PLATE I. *Begonia boliviensis* A. DC (Section BARYA A. DC)

Fig 1. Staminate flower x 1 5

Fig 2 Perianth of the staminate flower x 1.5.

Fig 3 Tepals of the staminate flower x 3
a - outer
b - inner

Fig 4. Androecium. x 3

Fig 5 Stamens x 9 5
a - back view
b - side view

Fig 6 Pistillate flower x 1

Fig. 7 Perianth of the pistillate flower x 1 5

Fig. 8. One of the tepals of the pistillate flower x 3.

Fig. 9 General view of the stigmas. x ca 5

Fig 10. A pair of stigmatic branches x 15

Fig. 11 Stigmatic surface x 60.

Fig 12 Ovary x 5

Fig. 13. Idem, cross section. x ca 8.
(Fig. 13 redrawn and enlarged from Curtis' Botanical Magazine, **93**: t 5657 1867.)

PLATE I

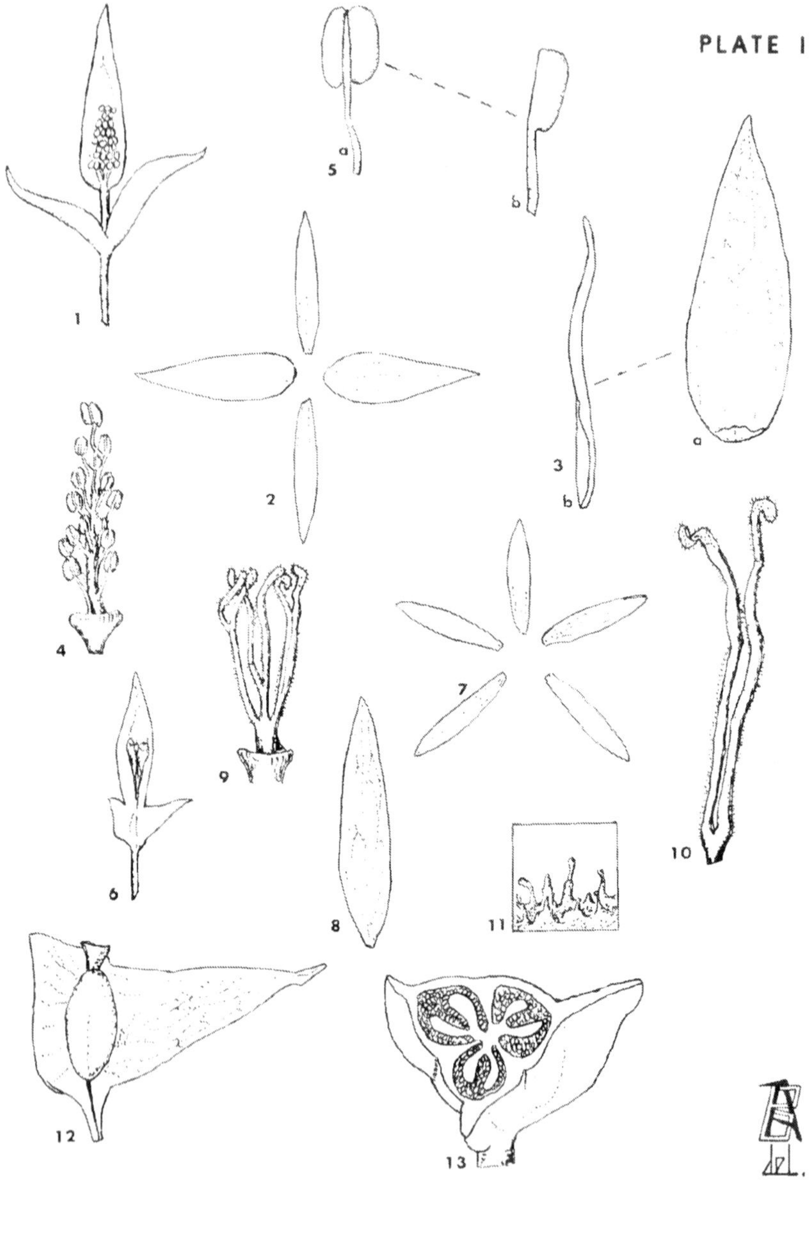

PLATE II *Begonia cucullata* Willd var *hookeri* Smith et Schubert
(Section BEGONIA)

Fig. 1. Staminate flower. x 2

Fig 2 Perianth of the staminate flower x 3.

Fig. 3. Tepals of the staminate flower x 3
a - outer
b - inner.

Fig. 4 Androecium x 5

Fig 5 Stamens x 10
a - outer stamen (short-filamented).
b - inner stamen (long-filamented)
c - abaxial side of a stamen showing discrete pollen sacks and overhanging connective
d - adaxial side of a stamen.

Fig. 6 Pistillate flower x 1 5

Fig. 7. One of the two bracteoles found at the base of the pedicel. x 4.

Fig. 8. One of the two bracteoles found at the base of the ovary x 5

Fig. 9. Perianth of the pistillate flower. x 3.

Fig 10 A pair of stigmatic branches x 8

Fig. 11 Stigmatic surface. x 60

Fig. 12 Ovary x 3

Fig 13 Idem, median cross section x 5

PLATE II

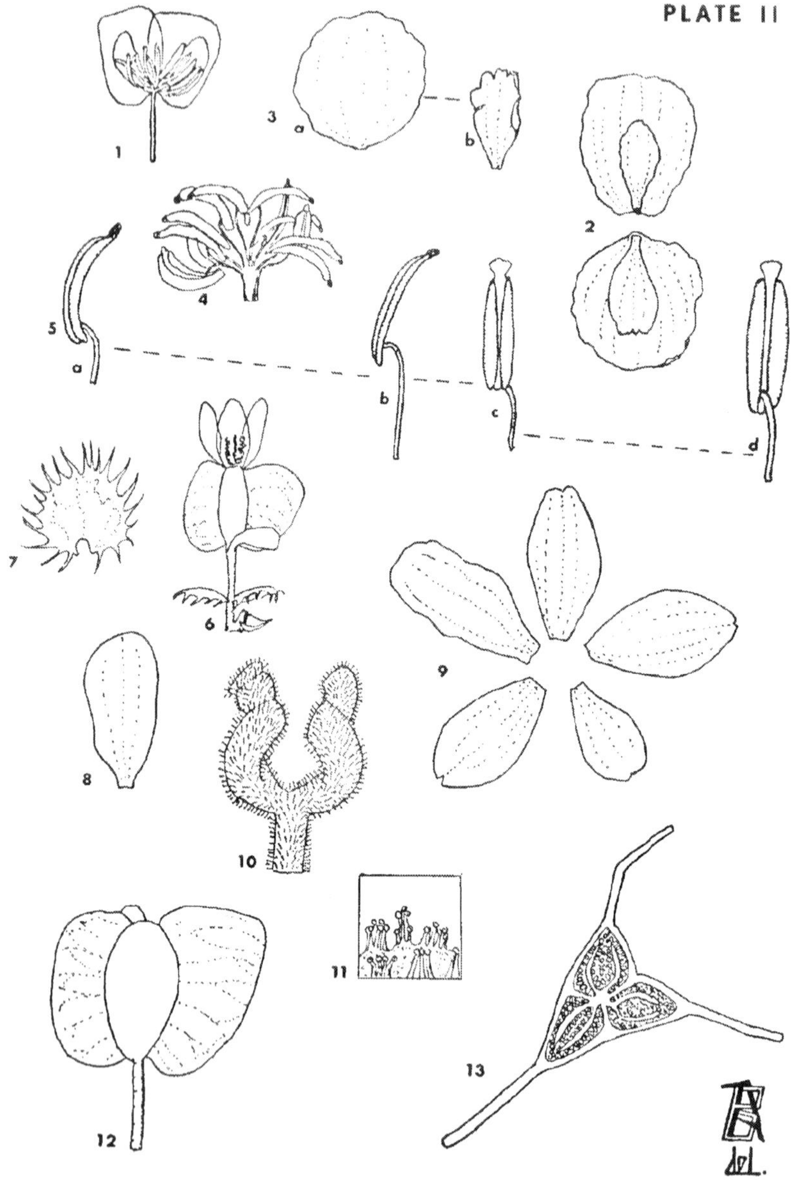

PLATE III *Begonia pseudo-lubbersii* Brade (Section BEGONIA)

Fig 1 Staminate flower x 1 5

Fig 2 Perianth of the staminate flower x 1.5

Fig 3 Tepals of the staminate flower x 1 7
a - outer
b - inner

Fig 4. Androecium x 5

Fig 5 Stamens x 10 (inner stamens long-filamented)

Fig 6. Pistillate flower. x 1 5

Fig 7 Perianth of the pistillate flower x 1 5

Fig. 8 General view of the styles and stigmas. x 10

Fig 9 Stigmatic surface. x 60

Fig 10. Ovary x 3

Fig 11. Idem, median cross section x 10

PLATE III

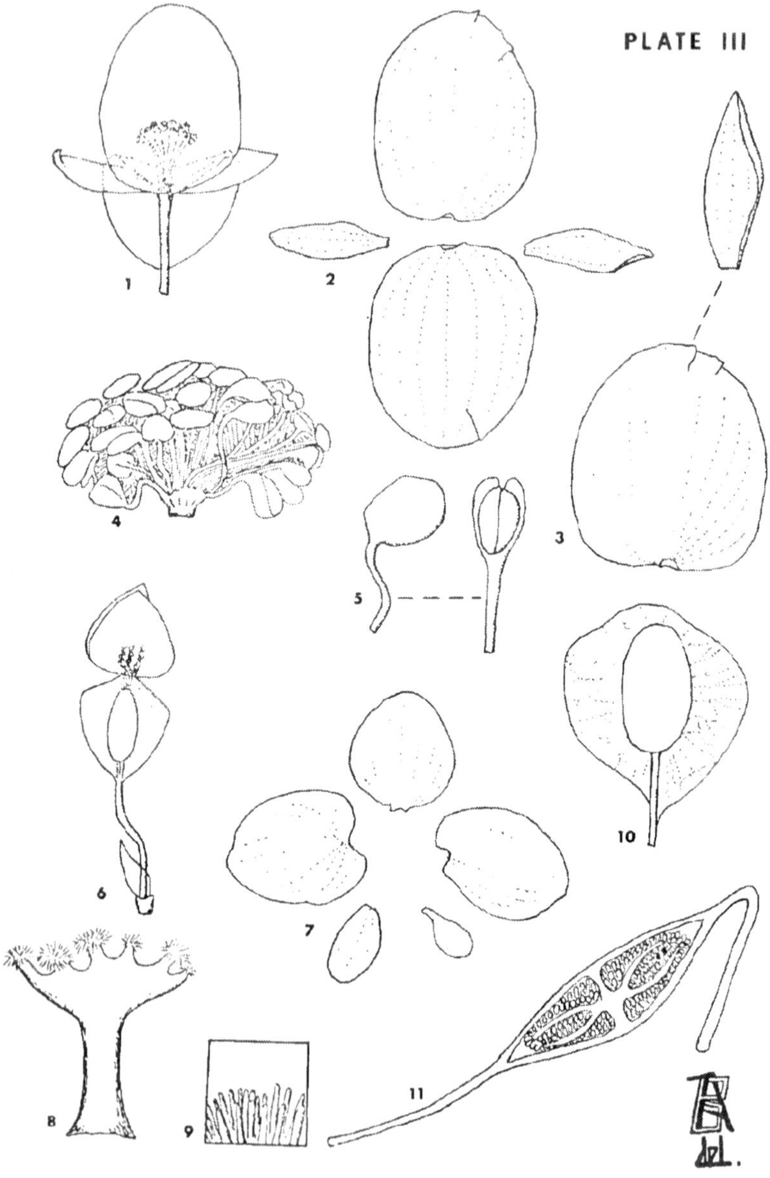

PLATE IV *Begonia schmidtiana* Regel (Section BEGONIA)

Fig 1 Staminate flower
a - flower bud x2
b - mature flower x 2.
c - portion of the pedicel showing trichomes x 10.

Fig 2 Perianth of the staminate flower (adaxial surface) x 3

Fig. 3 Tepals of the staminate flower x 4
a - outer (abaxial surface)
b - inner

Fig 4 Androecium. x 5

Fig. 5. Stamens. x 10

Fig 6. Pistillate flower. x 2

Fig. 7. Perianth of the pistillate flower. x 3.

Fig 8 A pair of stigmatic branches x 10

Fig 9. Stigmatic surface x 60

Fig. 10 Ovary x 5

Fig 11 Idem, median cross section x 10

PLATE IV

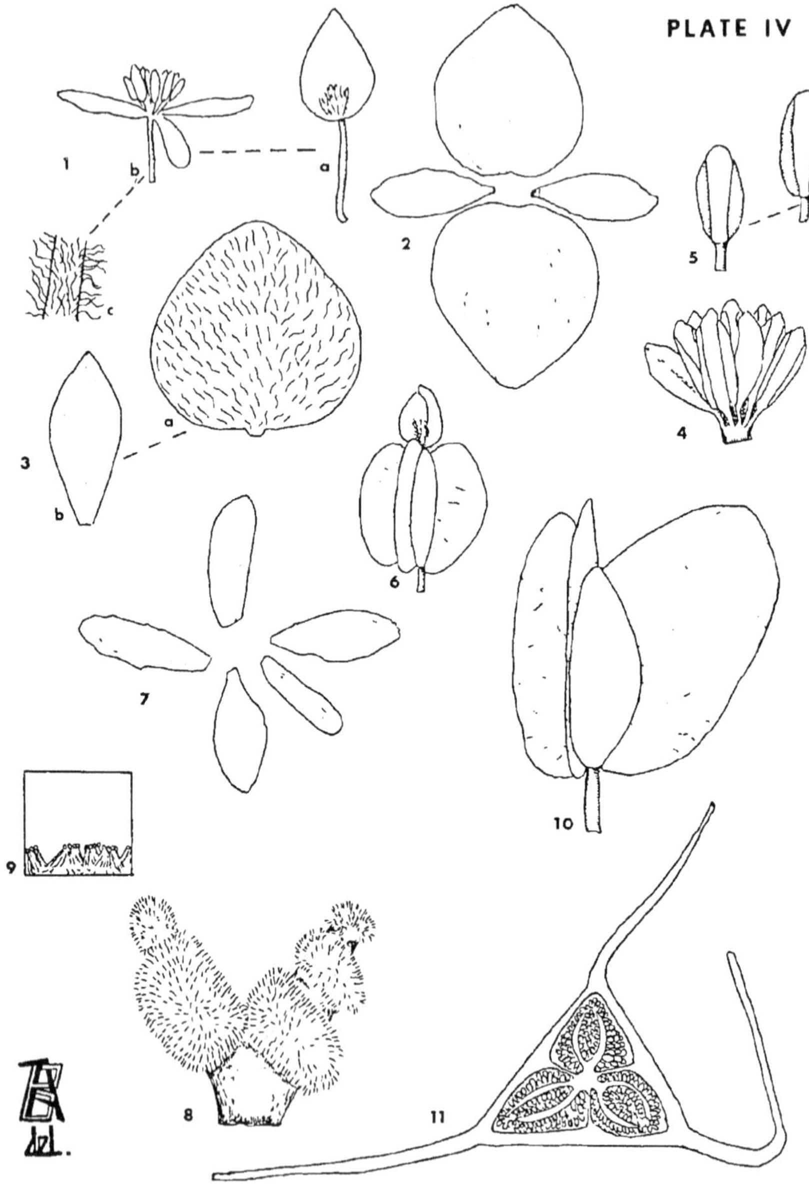

internal tepals lanceolate, 1 7 cm long, 0 6 cm broad, androecium 0 6 cm long, ca 1 cm broad, stamens 0.34 cm long (anthers 0 17 cm long, filaments 0 17 cm long), the inner ones with slightly longer filaments

Pistillate flower pedicel 2 5 cm long with one bracteole at the base, tepals five, 0 7 - 1 6 cm long, 0.4 - 1 4 cm broad, styles three, two-divided, branches very short, ca 0 03 cm long, stigmatic surface covers capitate endings of stigmatic branches, stigmatic papillae of the rod-like type, ovary two-celled, laterally compressed, 1 3 cm long, 0 5 cm broad, with two subequal wings ca 0 3 - 0 4 cm broad; placentae two-divided

(Note in the original description of the *Begonia pseudo-lubbersii* the ovary is described as three-celled, however, the ovary in the pistillate flower examined for this study was two-celled)

Begonia schmidtiana Regel, Descr Pl Nov et Minus Cognit Suppl p 880, Regel Gartenfl 28 321, t 990 1880 Plate IV.

Low semi-shrub, stems thick, branched below, branches red rough-haired, leaves obliquely cordate-ovate, palmately-7-9-veined, acute, duplicately crenate-dentate, subcoriaceous, on both surfaces rough-haired, dark green above, red beneath, 4.5 - 5 cm long, 3 cm broad, petioles red, rough-haired, longer than the blade, stipules ovate-oblong, ciliate, membranous, on the apex excurrent into a bristle.

Staminate flower pedicel 0 6 - 0 9 cm long, tepals four, at right angles with each other, external tepals 0.8 - 1.0 cm long, 0 7 - 0 8 cm broad, broadly cordate-ovate on the abaxial surface hairy, on the adaxial surface glabrous, internal tepals lanceolate, 0.8 cm long, 0.3 cm broad, glabrous on both sides, androecium 0 46 cm long, 0 6 cm broad, stamens 0 24 - 0.25 cm long, anthers 0.17 - 0 20 cm long, filaments 0 05 - 0 07 cm long, connective obtuse, a little overhanging

Pistillate flower pedicel 0 2 cm long, tepals five, oblong to oblong-lanceolate, 0 7 - 0.8 cm long, 0 4 - 1.0 cm broad, styles three, two-divided, branches ca 0.32 cm long, stigmatic surface forms helical bands with two to three twists, stigmatic papillae form conical, pyramid-like piles, ovary three-celled, 1.1 cm long, 0.32 cm broad, placentae two-divided

Section CASPARYA (Klotzsch)
A.DC , Prodr **15**, 1 269 1864

Staminate flower tepals four, filaments free, anthers linear, connective often broad, overhanging

Pistillate flower tepals five to six, styles three, often persistent for a long time, two-divided with the branches which are again divided many times, branches erect, covered around with stigmatic papillae, placentae two-divided, coming out from the inner corners of the cells, fruit three-celled, only seldom provided with clearly defined wings, for this reason it is mostly simply triquetrous with each of the edges terminating in a horn, dehiscing at maturity on the edges.

Erect (or probably scrambling or partly climbing) semi-shrubs with pinnately veined leaves.

Type species *Begonia urticae* L *f*

Species examined *Begonia fuchsiaeflora* (A DC.) A Baranov and Barkley

Begonia fuchsiaeflora (A.DC.) A Baranov
and Barkley, Phytologia **26**. 217-220. 1973 Plate V

Branches herbaceous, glabrous, leaves ovate, acuminate, cordate at the base, with one of the basal lobes larger than another, glabrous above, hairy along the veins on the underside, denticulate and setose along the margin, petioles glabrous, stipules dimidiate-obovate, mucronate, glabrous, inflorescence almost equal to leaves, branches many times forked, erect, glabrous, bracts oblong, laciniate-setose on the apex

Staminate flower pedicel 0 3 cm long, tepals four, cross-wise oppositely arranged, external tepals 0 9 - 1 0 cm long, 0 62 - 0 70 cm broad, subelongate cordate-ovate at the base with rolled inwards margins, androecium 0 41 cm long, 0 41 cm broad, stamens of two kinds, outer short-filamented (anthers 0.19 cm long, filaments 0 12 cm long), inner long-filamented (anthers 0 15 cm long, filaments 0 20 cm long), connective broad, obtuse, overhanging a little

Pistillate flower: pedicel 1 7 cm long, tepals five, oblong, obovate or ovate-lanceolate, 0 9 - 1 2 cm long, 0 45 - 0 70 cm broad, styles three, two-divided, branches twisted, ca. 0 20 cm long, covered on all sides with stigmatic papillae, stigmatic papillae papilliform or in a form of low conelets, ovary three-celled, 0 9 cm long, 0 4 cm broad, wings three, unequal, the largest one 0.65 cm broad, the other two 0 23 - 0.28 cm broad, placentae split into two narrow lobes

Section DORATOMETRA (Klotzsch)
A.DC , Prodomus **15**, 1 383 1864

Staminate flower tepals two or four; filaments free or united below, anthers ovate or oblong, obtuse, somewhat longer than the filaments, connective overhanging a little

Pistillate flower tepals four to five, styles three, persistent, scarcely united below, two-divided, branches linear, stigmatic papillae form a

PLATE V *Begonia fuchsiaeflora* (A DC) Barkley *et* A Baranov (Section CASPARYA Warb)

Fig 1 Staminate flower x 3

Fig 2. Perianth of the staminate flower x 4

Fig 3 Tepals of the staminate flower.
a - outer x 4
b - inner x 4.

Fig 4. Androecium x 10

Fig 5 Stamens
a - outer stamen (short-filamented). x 10.
b - inner stamen (long-filamented) x 10.

Fig. 6. Pistillate flower x 2

Fig. 7 Bracteole of the pistillate flower. x 3

Fig 8 Perianth of the pistillate flower x 2

Fig 9. A pair of stigmatic branches x 10.

Fig 10 Stigmatic surface x 60

Fig. 11. Ovary x 4

Fig 12 Idem, median cross section x 10

PLATE V

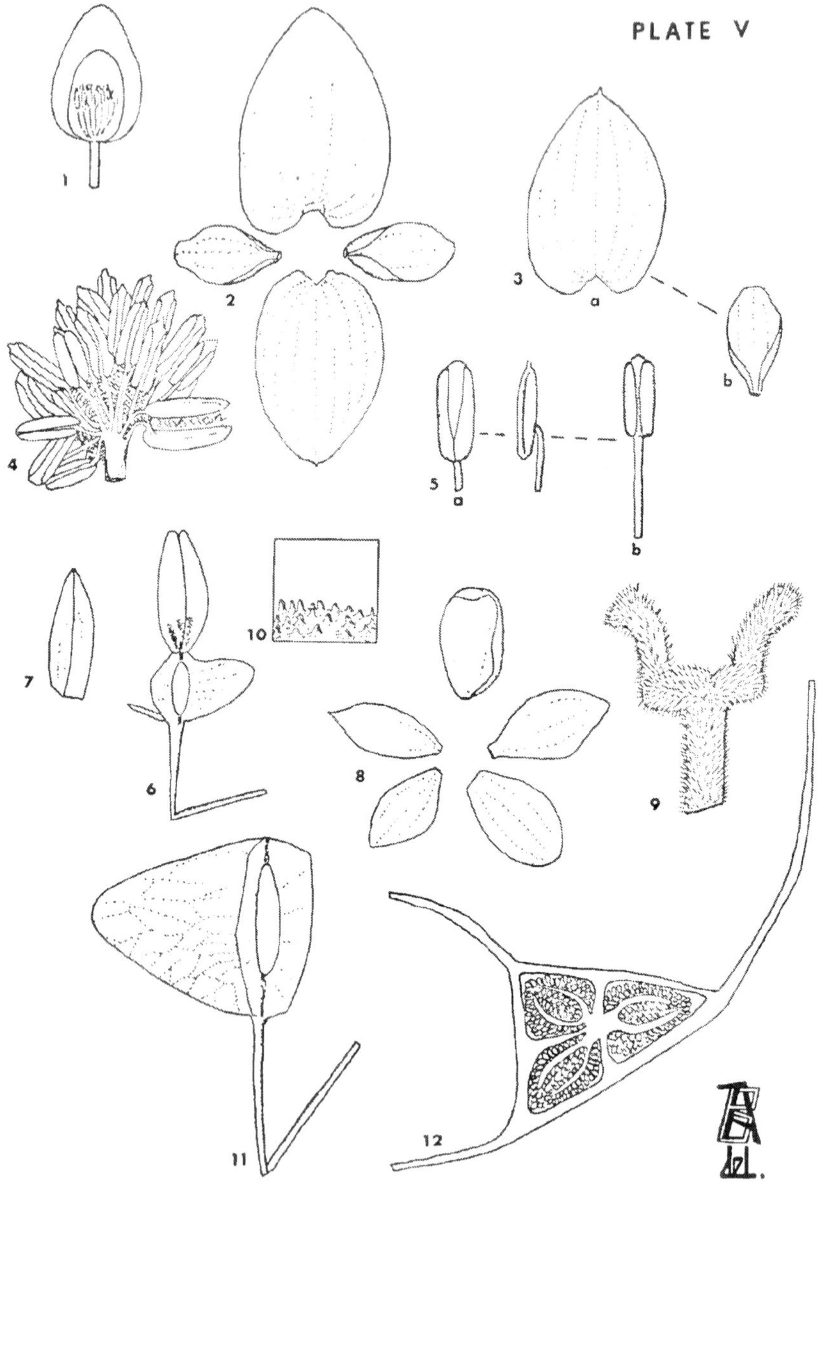

PLATE VI *Begonia franconis* Liebm (Section DORATOMETRA A.DC.)

Fig 1 Staminate flower
a - general outer view x 2
b - portion of the pedicel showing trichomes x 15.

Fig 2. Perianth of the staminate flower (adaxial surface) x 3

Fig. 3. Tepals of the staminate flower
a - outer (abaxial surface) x 3
b - inner. x 3

Fig. 4. Androecium x 5

Fig 5. Stamens x 20

Fig. 6 Pistillate flower.
a - general outer view. x 1 5
b - portion of the pedicel showing trichomes x 5

Fig. 7 Perianth of the pistillate flower x 3

Fig. 8 General view of the stigmas x 10

Fig 9 Stigmatic surface x 60.

Fig. 10. Ovary. x 5

Fig. 11 Idem, median cross section
a - general view. x 10.
b - one locule showing placenta and ovules. x ca 20

PLATE VI

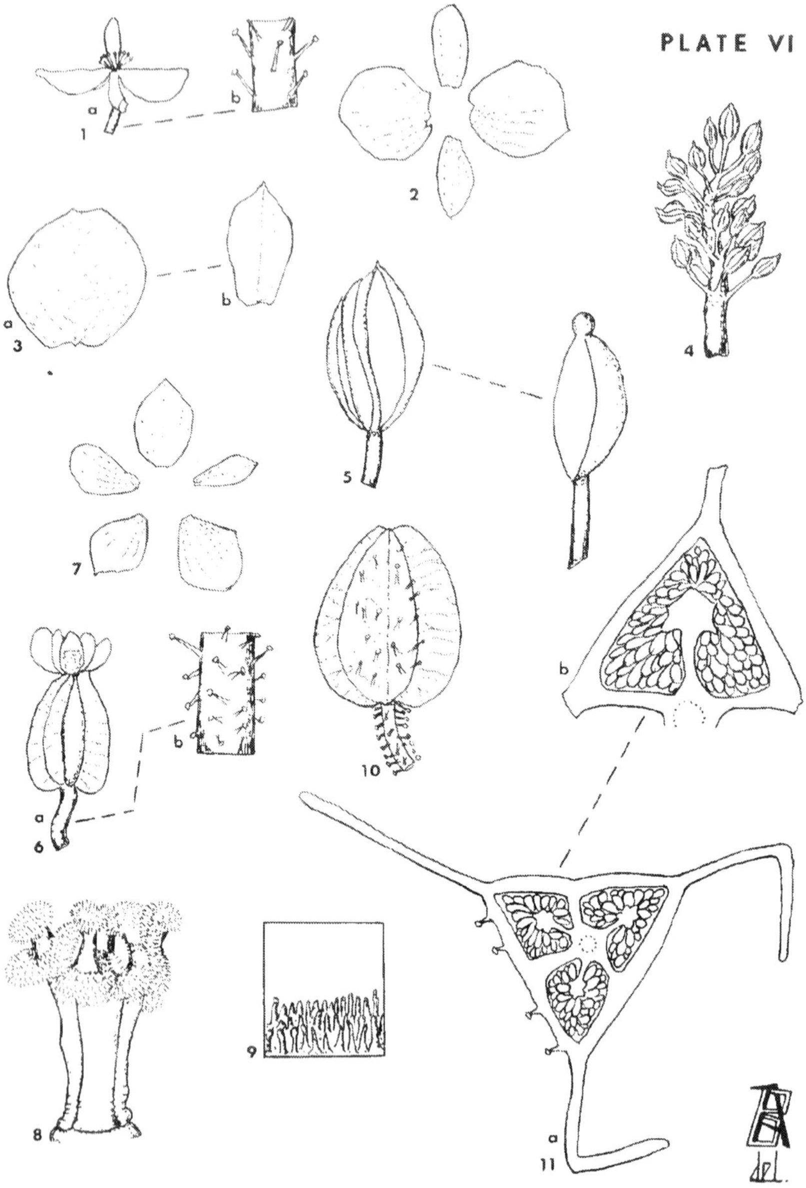

continuous helical band with one to two turns, placentae undivided (or only as an exception divided in only one of the cells), fruit three-celled, wings three, subequal.

Erect herbs with slender stems, palmately veined leaves and lateral few-flowered inflorescences, bracts very small, sometimes persistent

Type species *Begonia wallichiana* Steudel

Species examined *Begonia franconis* Liebmann

Begonia franconis Liebmann, Kjoeb.
Vidensk. Meddel. 21 1853 Plate VI

Annual, covered with viscid hairs, stem erect, low, leaves obliquely ovate, acute, palmately-7-8-veined, subcordate at the base, irregularly crenulate-dentate, on both sides shortly hairy and in addition covered with scattered bristles; stipules ovate, acute, ciliate, persistent, inflorescence much shorter than the leaves, few flowered, dichasial, producing both kinds of flowers.

Staminate flower· pedicel 0 5 cm long; tepals four, at right angles with each other, external tepals irregularly ovate-orbiculate, 0 85 - 0 90 cm long, 0 90 - 0 93 cm broad, on the abaxial surface hairy, on the adaxial surface glabrous, internal tepals oblong or oblong-lanceolate, 0 7 - 0 8 cm long, 0 33 - 0 43 cm broad, on both sides glabrous, androecium 1 44 cm long, 0 6 cm broad, stamens 0 15 - 0 28 cm long, arising on all sides and on different levels of a cylindrical column, anthers 0 14 - 0 15 cm long, filaments 0.01 - 0.13 cm long, connective overhanging

Pistillate flower pedicel 1.0 cm long, tepals five, elliptic to obovate, 0 6 - 0 8 cm long, 0 3 - 0 6 cm broad, styles three, twice divided, branches erect, ca 0 18 cm long, stigmatic surface forms helical bands with one-two turns, stigmatic papillae in form of capitate glandular hairs, ovary three-celled, 1.2 cm long, 0.16 cm broad, beset with glandular hairs, wings three, subequal, ca 0 20 cm broad, placentae non-divided, rounded in outline, on the margins lobate.

Section ENITA Brade,
Rodriguesia **32**.160 1957

Staminate flower stamens slightly united below, anthers usually much shorter than the filaments

Pistillate flower: stigmas two-divided, over the whole surface beset with papillae, ovary three-celled; placentae simple (non-divided); seeds cylindrical, at the apex crowned with a group of larger cells in a cap-like fashion.

Climbing semi-shrubs, stem rooting at the internodes, leaves symmetrical or subsymmetrical, pinnately or palmately-veined, or two to four-lobed and palmately veined

Typical species: *Begonia convolvulacea* A.DC and *B fagifolia* Fischer in Otto *et* Dietrich.

Species examined *Begonia convolvulacea* A DC

Begonia convolvulacea A.DC *in* Martius,
Fl Braz **4**,1:367. 1861 Plate VII.

Climbing, branched, glabrous, stem rooting at the nodes, leaves rotundate-angulate, palmately-4-7-veined, subcordate, with three to five acuminate, unequal, angulate lobes, undulate-crenate along the margin; stipules ovate-oblong, acute, inflorescence axillary, dichasial, longer than the leaves

Staminate flower pedicel 0.9 cm long, tepals four cross-wise oppositely arranged, external tepals broad ovate, acuminate, 0 6 cm long, 0.5 cm broad, inner tepals oblong, slightly acuminate, 0 6 cm long, 0 3 cm broad, androecium 0 5 cm long, 0.8 cm broad, stamens of two kinds, outer or short-filamented (anthers 0 14 cm long, filaments 0.09 cm long) and inner or long-filamented (anthers 0 16 cm long, filaments 0 17 cm long), connective broad, obtuse or acutish, overhanging a little.

Pistillate flower pedicel 0 6 cm long, tepals five, elliptic or oblong, sometimes acuminate or with rolled inwards (involute) margins, 0 4 - 0.5 cm long, 0.20 - 0.35 cm broad, styles three, two-divided, branches twisted, ca 0 25 cm long, stigmatic papillae in form of low conelets, covering stigmatic branches on all sides, ovary three-celled, 0.5 cm long, 0.28 cm broad, wings three, strongly unequal, the largest one 0.6 cm broad, the two others 0 03 - 0 05 cm broad, placentae non-divided, ovate in outline.

<u>Section GAERDTIA (Klotzsch) A.DC.,
Ann Sci Nat. Bot 4,**11** 128. 1859</u>

Staminate flower tepals four, filaments free, affixed to a somewhat convex torus, anthers obovate or oblong-obovate, opening by longitudinal slits.

Pistillate flower: tepals five, styles three, later falling off, two-divided, stigmatic papillae form a continuous helical band with one to two turns, placentae two-divided and the two placental lobes in each cell cling to each other so that the ovules arise only on their outer sides; fruit three-celled, wings three, sub-equal.

Glabrous semi-shrubs with pinnately or palmate-pinnately veined leaves. Inflorescence axillary, not very many flowered

PLATE VII *Begonia convolvulacea* A DC (Section ENITA Brade)

Fig 1 Staminate flower, general outer view x 3

Fig 2 Perianth of the staminate flower x 4

Fig 3 Tepals of the staminate flower
a - outer x 4
b - inner x 4

Fig 4 Androecium x 5

Fig 5 Stamens.
a - short-filamented (outer) x 10.
b - long-filamented (inner) stamen x 10

Fig 6 Pistillate flower, general outer view x 3

Fig 7. Perianth of the pistillate flower x 5

Fig 8 A pair of stigmatic branches. x 10.

Fig. 9 Stigmatic surface x 60

Fig. 10 Ovary x 5.

Fig 11 Idem, median cross section x 10

PLATE VII

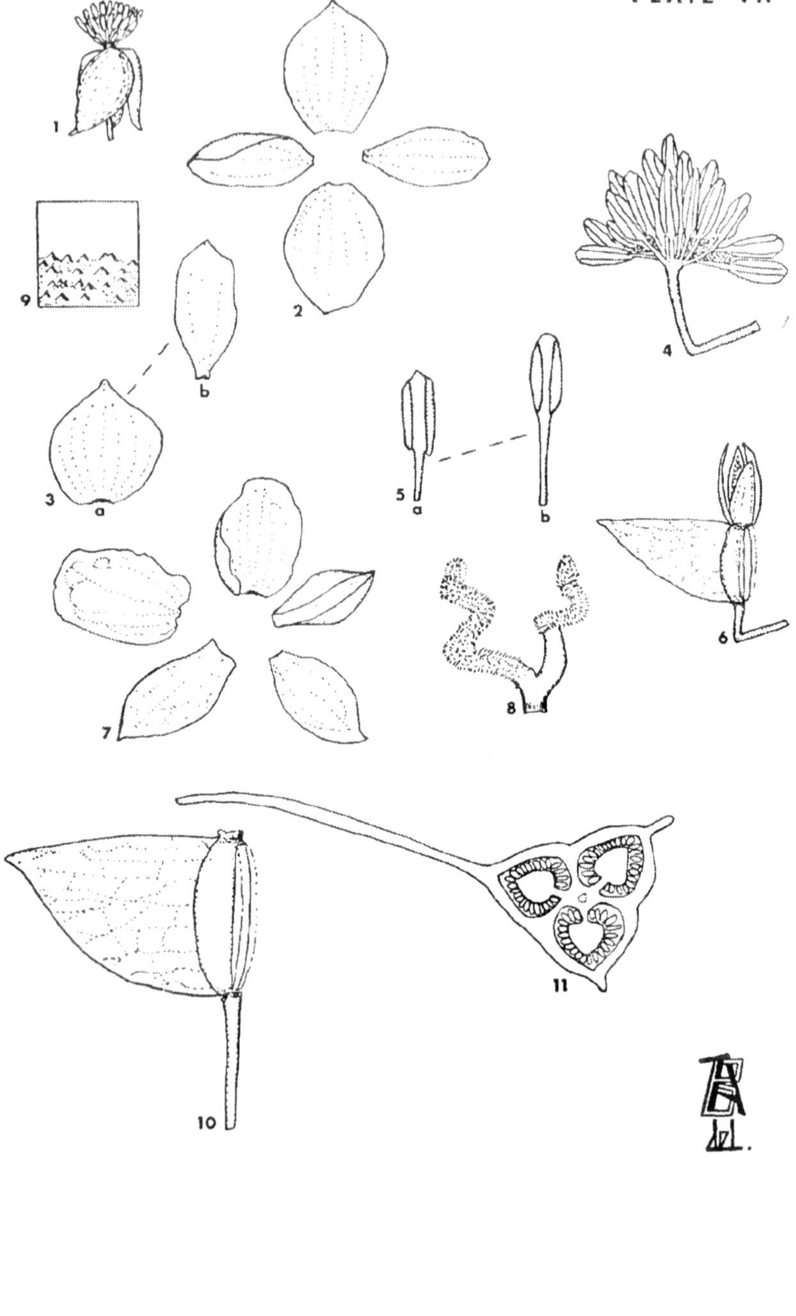

PLATE VIII *Begonia maculata* Raddi (Section GAERDTIA A DC)

Fig 1. Staminate flower
a - general outer view x 1.5.
b - portion of the pedicel showing trichomes x 7.

Fig. 2 Perianth of the staminate flower x 1 8

Fig 3. Tepals of the staminate flower
a - outer x 3
b - inner. x 3

Fig. 4 Androecium x 3

Fig. 5 Idem, longitudinal section. x 7.5.

Fig 6. Stamens x 9 5.

Fig 7 Pistillate flower. x 1.5.

Fig 8. Perianth of the pistillate flower. x 1.5

Fig. 9. Tepals of the pistillate flower x 3

Fig 10 A pair of stigmatic branches x 9 5.

Fig 11 Stigmatic surface x 60.

Fig 12. Ovary x 5.

Fig 13. Idem, median cross section x 16

PLATE VIII

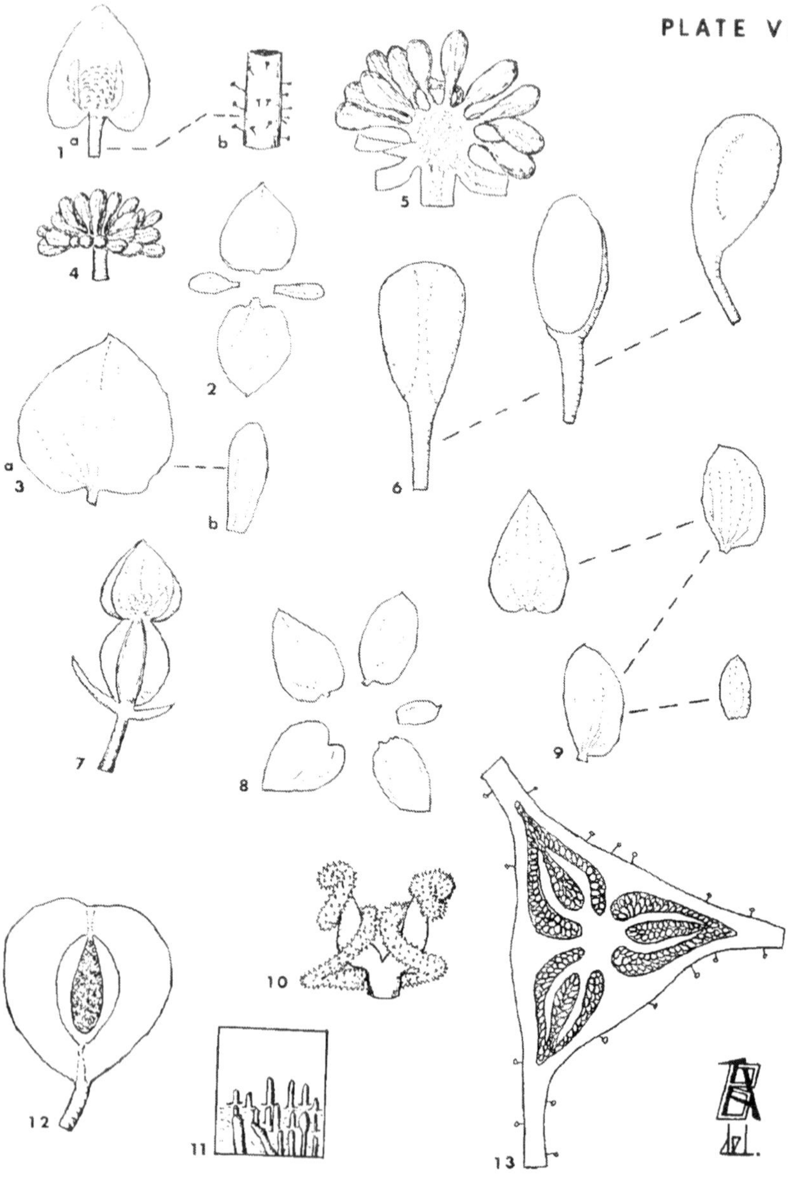

Type species. *Begonia maculata* Raddi

Species examined *Begonia maculata* Raddi

Begonia maculata Raddi, Mem Mod
18 t 406 1820 Plate VIII

Small, glabrous shrub, leaves obliquely ovate-oblong, acute, cordate at the base, coriaceous, mostly white-spotted above, more or less purple-red beneath, stipules elongate-lanceolate, acuminate, caducous, inflorescence axillary, dichasial, more often nodding, producing both kinds of flowers

Staminate flower: pedicel 0 6 cm long, tepals four, at right angles with each other, external tepals broadly cordate, 1.5 - 1 6 cm long, 1 3 - 1 5 cm broad, internal tepals 0 7 - 0 8 cm long, 0 15 - 0.27 cm broad, spatulate or linear-obovate, androecium 0.55 cm long, 0 65 cm broad, stamens 0 30 cm long, anthers 0 15 - 0 20 cm long, filaments 0 10 - 0 15 cm long, connective not overhanging

Pistillate flower pedicel 0 6 cm long, with two bracteoles at the base of the ovary, tepals five, ovate to obliquely ovate-elliptic, 0.70 - 1 15 cm long, 0 30 - 0 70 cm broad, styles three, twice divided, branches suberect, 0.2 cm long; stigmatic surface in a form of a continuous helical band with two turns on each pair of the branches, stigmatic papillae of a rod-like type, ovary three-celled, 1.05 cm long, 0 4 cm broad, wings three, equal, placentae divided into two narrow lobes

(Note According to literature dealing with members of this section, placental lobes in each cell cling to each other so that the ovules are produced only on their outer sides In the ovary of *Begonia maculata* Raddi examined for this study placental lobes had ovules on both sides)

Section HAAGEA (Klotzsch) A DC., Prodromus **15**,1:391 1864.

Staminate flower tepals two, filaments free, affixed to a slightly convex torus, anthers oblong, obtuse, approximately as long as the filaments, connective not overhanging.

Pistillate flower tepals two, styles three, later falling off, almost not united at all below, two-divided; branches diverging; stigmatic papillae form a continuous helical band, placentae not divided, fruit three-celled, with three subequal wings.

Erect semi-shrubs with palmate-pinnately veined, short-petioled leaves, inflorescence axillary, not very many-flowered.

Type species: *Begonia dipetala* R. Graham *in* Hooker.

Species examined *Begonia dipetala* R Graham *in* Hooker.

Begonia dipetala R Graham *in* Hooker,
Bot Mag **55** t 2849. 1828. Plate IX.

Subglabrous, erect shrub, leaves obliquely ovate, acute, semi-cordate at the base, palmate-pinnately-7-9-veined, duplicately dentate, on both sides sparsely bristle-bearing, stipules ovate-oblong, mucronate, membranous, caducous; inflorescence shorter than leaves, nodding, branches many times divided, bracts ovate-oblong, acute, caducous

Staminate flower pedicel 1 2 cm long, tepals two, suborbiculate, slightly cordate at the base, 1 2 - 1 3 cm long, 1 4 - 1.5 cm broad, androecium 0 80 cm long, 0.85 cm broad, stamens 0.4 - 0 5 cm long, anthers 0 10 - 0 25 cm long, filaments 0 25 - 0.30 cm long, connective broad, obtuse, slightly overhanging

Pistillate flower. pedicel 1 0 cm long, tepals two, obliquely suborbiculate-cordate, 1 0 - 1.3 cm long, 1 5 - 1 65 cm broad; styles three, two-divided, branches diverging, very short, 0.16 - 0.18 cm long, stigmatic surface forms continuous helical bands with one turn, stigmatic papillae of a pinnacle-like type, ovary three-celled, 1.6 cm long, 0 35 cm broad, wings three, subequal, ca. 0 21 - 0 28 cm broad, placentae non-divided, acutely lobed.

Section HUSZIA (Klotzsch)
A DC., Ann Sci. Nat. Bot. 4,**11** 121. 1859

Staminate flower tepals four to eight; filaments free, affixed to a slightly convex torus, anthers obovate or oblong, connective sometimes overhanging a little

Pistillate flower: tepals four to six (usually five), styles three, mostly persistent, shortly united below, two-divided, stigmatic papillae form a continuous helical band, placentae two-divided, sometimes placental segments are lobed again, fruit three-celled, with one large wing

Annual, mostly stemless, herbs, with persistent, thick basal tuber; leaves long-petioled, palmately veined, often peltate, scarcely oblique, inflorescence many-flowered, large, with particularly large flowers

Type species *Begonia octopetala* l'Heritier

Species examined *Begonia monophylla* Pavon *ex* A DC

Begonia monophylla Pavon *ex* A.DC.,
Ann Sci Nat. Ser 4,**11**.121 1859 Plate X

Stemless, leaf one, broadly orbiculate, peltately or palmately-12-15-veined, undulate, denticulate, pilose on both sides, petiole pilose,

PLATE IX *Begonia dipetala* R. Graham *in* Hooker (Section HAAGEA A DC)

Fig 1 Staminate flower x 1 5.

Fig 2 Perianth of the staminate flower. x 1 5

Fig 3. One of the tepals of the staminate flower x 3

Fig. 4 Androecium. x 5

Fig. 5. Stamens. x 10

Fig 6 Pistillate flower. x 1 5

Fig 7. Perianth of the pistillate flower x 3

Fig. 8 General view of the stigmas. x 10

Fig 9. Stigmatic surface x 60

Fig 10 Ovary x 2 5.

Fig. 11 Idem, median cross section.
a - general view x 10.
b - one locule showing placenta and ovules x ca 20

PLATE IX

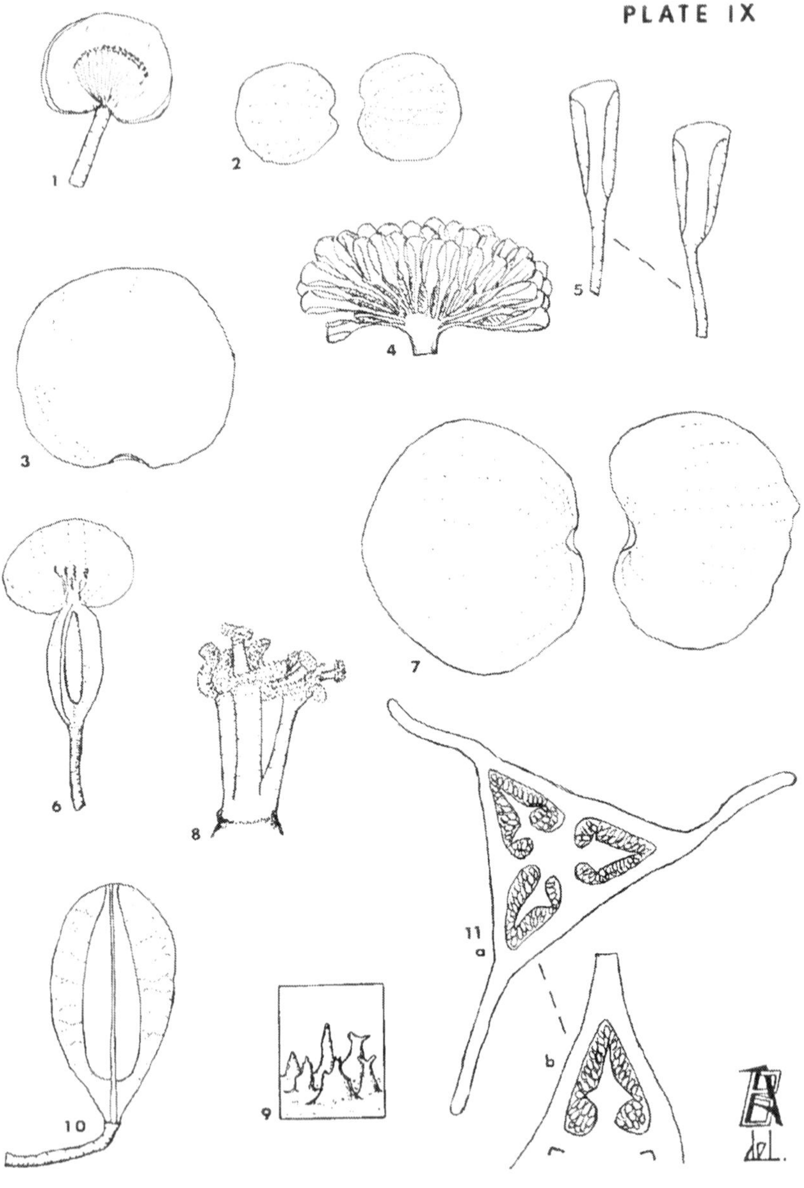

PLATE X *Begonia monophylla* Pavon *ex* A DC (Section HUSZIA A DC)

Fig 1 Staminate flower
a - general outer view x 1 5.
b - portion of the pedicel showing trichomes x 7 5

Fig 2 Perianth of the staminate flower x 1 5

Fig 3 Tepals of the staminate flower
a - outer. x 3.
b - inner. x 3

Fig. 4 Androecium. x 3.

Fig. 5 Idem, longitudinal section x 5

Fig. 6 Stamens (basal portions of the filaments removed) x 7 5

Fig 7 Pistillate flower. x 1 5.

Fig. 8 Bracteole of the pistillate flower. x 5

Fig 9. Perianth of the pistillate flower x 1 5

Fig 10 General view of the stigmas x 7 5.

Fig 11 A pair of stigmatic branches x 15

Fig. 12. Stigmatic surface x 60

Fig. 13 Ovary x 5

Fig. 14 Idem, median cross section x 12

PLATE X

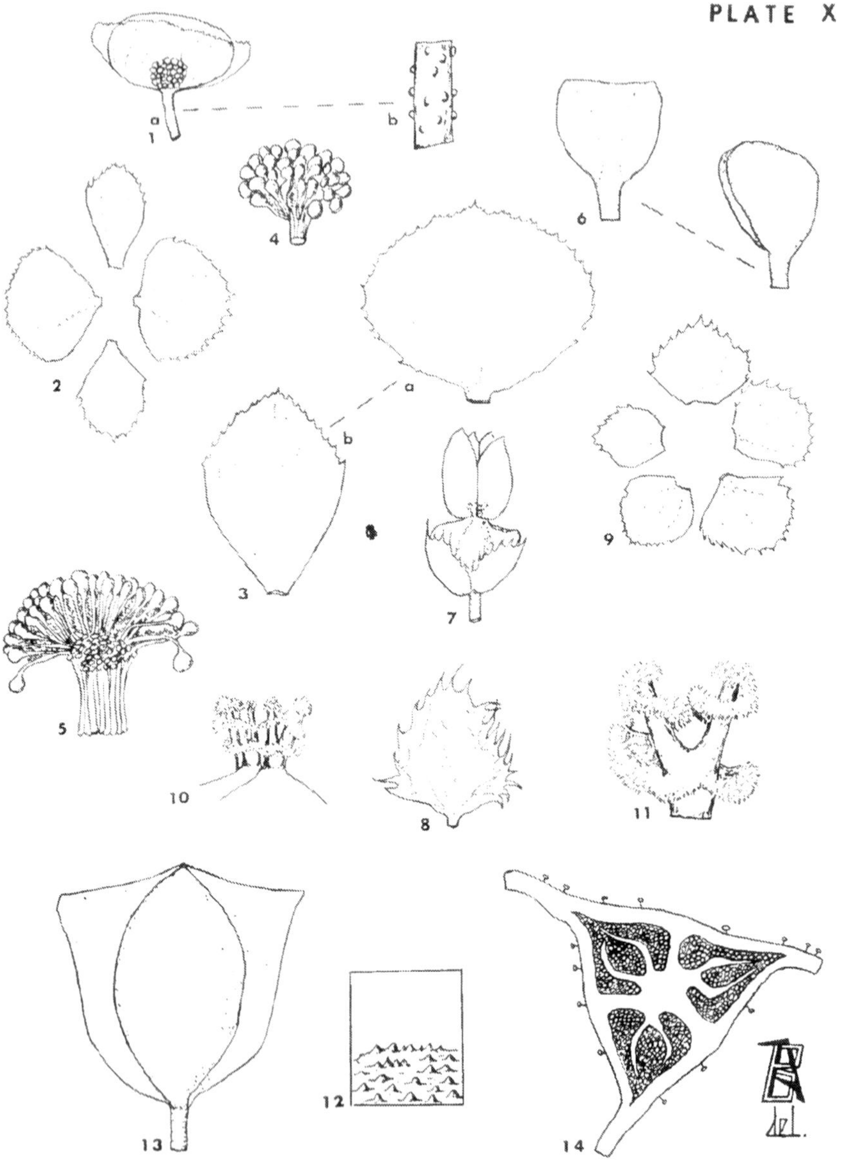

PLATE XI *Begonia foliosa* HBK (Section LEPSIA A DC)

Fig 1 Staminate flower x 3

Fig. 2. Perianth of the staminate flower x 3.

Fig. 3 Tepals of the staminate flower
a - outer x 3
b - inner. x 3.

Fig 4 Androecium x 7

Fig. 5. Stamens. x 10

Fig. 6. Pistillate flower. x 3.

Fig 7. Perianth of the pistillate flower x 3.

Fig. 8 General view of the stigmas x 10

Fig. 9 Stigmatic surface x 60

Fig. 10. Ovary. x 4

Fig 11. Idem, median cross section. x 10.

PLATE XI

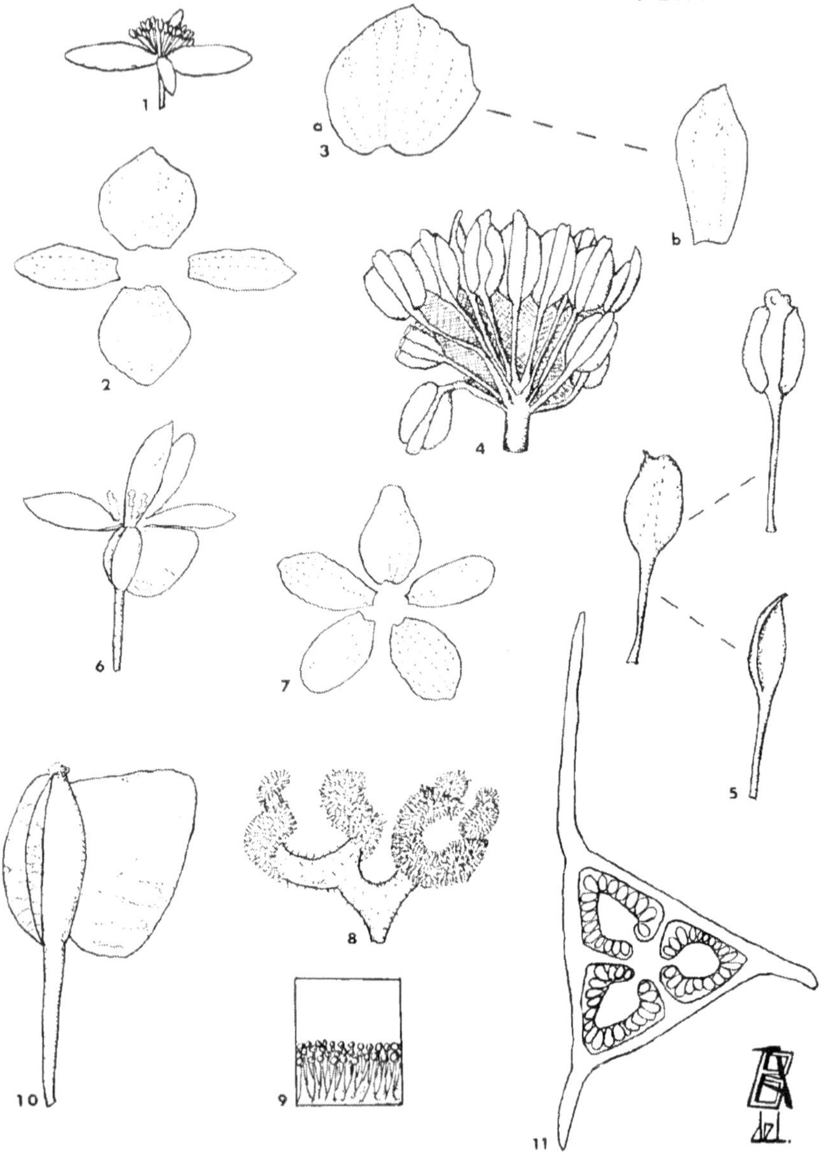

inflorescence much longer than the leaves, peduncle pilose on the apex two or three times forked, bracts broadly ovate, laciniate, persistent

Staminate flower pedicel 1.0 cm long, tepals four, at right angles with each other, external tepals very broadly ovate to obovate, serrulate along the margin, 1 8 - 1 9 cm long, 2 1 - 2 3 cm broad, internal tepals obovate, in the upper half serrulate along the margin, 1.8 - 1.9 cm long, 2.1 - 2 3 cm broad, internal tepals obovate, in the upper half serrulate along the margin, 1 8 - 2.0 cm long, 1 2 - 1 3 cm broad, androecium 0 7 cm long, 0 7 cm broad, stamens united below, in the free part 0 5 cm long, anthers 0.25 - 0.30 cm long, filaments 0 15 - 0.20 cm long, connective not overhanging

Pistillate flower pedicel 0 7 cm long, with two laciniate-setose bracteoles at the base of the ovary, tepals five, very broadly ovate to obovate, in the upper half denticulate along the margin, 0.95 - 1 15 cm long, 0 80 - 1 25 cm broad, styles three, twice divided, branches diverging, ca. 0 13 cm long, stigmatic surface forms helical bands with one to two twists, stigmatic papillae in form of small conelets, ovary three-celled, 0.95 cm long, 0 5 cm broad, wings three, subequal, ca 0 16 cm broad, placentae two-divided into narrow lobes

(Note According to the existing descriptions of this section, its members have fruits with one large wing. The specimen of an ovary of this species, examined for this study, had three subequal wings)

Section LEPSIA (Klotzsch) A DC., Ann Sci. Nat Bot 4,11 139. 1859

Staminate flower tepals four, filaments united below, anthers ovate, somewhat acute, longer than the filaments, connective overhanging

Pistillate flower tepals five, styles three, united below, mostly persistent, stigmatic branches twisted, stigmatic papillae form a continuous helical band with three turns, placentae non-divided, fruit three-celled, with three unequal wings.

Slightly climbing shrubs with slender stems, small, short-petioled, pinnately veined leaves without cystoliths, and membranous, persistent stipules and bracts, inflorescence few-flowered, axillary

Type species *Begonia foliosa* HBK.

Species examined. *Begonia foliosa* HBK.

Begonia foliosa HBK , Nov Gen. et Sp. 7 183, t.642. 1825 Plate XI.

Climbing, richly branched, glabrous semi-shrub, branchlets many-leaved;

leaves subsessile, obliquely oblong, acute, semi-cordate, sharply serrate, underneath papillose, veins obsolete, stipules petiolate, paired, obliquely ovate, acutely-subaristate, completely entire, very thin, membranous, glabrous, persistent.

Staminate flower pedicel 0.5 cm long, tepals four, crosswise oppositely arranged, external tepals very broadly cordate-ovate, 0 90 - 0.95 cm long, 0.90 - 0.93 cm broad, internal tepals oblong, 1 0 - 1 03 cm long, 0 40 - 0 43 cm broad, androecium 0 5 cm long, 0.7 cm broad, stamens 0.30 - 0 45 cm long, anthers 0 19 - 0 21 cm long, filaments 0.09 - 0 26 cm long, connective sometimes moderately overhanging

Pistillate flower pedicel 0 8 cm long, tepals five, oblong or obliquely oblong-elliptic or oblong-ovate, 0.8 - 1.0 cm long, 0 40 - 0 60 cm broad; styles three, two-divided, with curved branches, ca 0.24 cm long, stigmatic surface forms continuous helical bands with two turns, stigmatic papillae in the form of capitate glandular hairs; ovary three-celled, 0 65 cm long, 0 38 cm broad, wings three, strongly unequal, the largest one 0 48 cm broad, the other two 0.08 - 0.15 cm broad, placentae non-divided ovate in outline

Section PETERMANNIA (Klotzsch) A DC , Ann Sci. Nat Bot. 4,**11**:128. 1859

Staminate flower tepals two, filaments mostly affixed in a more or less circular fashion in a conoidal column, anthers obovate, approximately of the length of the filaments.

Pistillate flower· tepals five, styles three, two-divided, not persistent, stigmatic papillae form continuous helical bands, placentae two divided, fruit three-celled, with three subequal wings

Mostly erect semishrubs with pinnately or palmate-pinnately veined leaves, inflorescences terminal or opposite to the leaves, paniculate or few-flowered

Type species. *Begonia cumingiana* A.DC

Species examined *Begonia boisiana* Gagnepain

Begonia boisiana Gagnepain, Bull.Mus Hist Nat Paris **25** 195. 1919. Plate XII.

Caulescent, herbaceous plant, stem erect, branched, with swollen nodes, leaves narrow ovate or lanceolate, rounded or rather cordate at the base, with unequal basal lobes, obliquely acuminate, coarsely and remotely dentate, shining above, purple, especially along the veins beneath, veins eight, rather pinnate or pinnate-palmate, petioles strongly unequal, the uppermost are the shortest, stipules ovate, on the apex finely awned, moderately caducous, inflorescences

PLATE XII. *Begonia boisiana* Gagnepain (Section PETERMANNIA A.DC)

Fig 1 Staminate flower x 2

Fig. 2. Perianth of the staminate flower x 3

Fig. 3. Tepals of the staminate flower
a - outer x 5
b - inner x 5

Fig 4. Androecium x 10

Fig. 5. Stamens.
a - inner stamen (long-filamented) x 15
b - outer stamen (short-filamented) x 15
c - ventral view of the anther x 20

Fig 6. Pistillate flower x 3.

Fig. 7. Portion of the pedicel of the pistillate flower showing trichomes. x 25

Fig 8. Perianth of the pistillate flower x 4

Fig 9. A pair of stigmatic branches. x 30

Fig 10. Stigmatic surface x 60

Fig. 11. Ovary x 5

Fig. 12 Idem, median cross section. x 10

PLATE XII

terminal cymous, pedicels slender, bracts imitating the form of stipules, small, flowers pink or whitish

Staminate flower pedicel 0 65 cm long, tepals four, at right angles with each other, external tepals very broadly ovate, sometimes at the base with involute margins, 0.7 - 0 8 cm long, 0 70 - 0 75 cm broad, internal tepals oblong-lanceolate, 0.80 - 0 86 cm long, 0 30 - 0.35 cm broad, androecium 0.32 cm long, 0 44 cm broad, stamens of two kinds, outer or short-filamented (anthers 0 06 cm long, filaments 0 12 cm long) and inner or long-filamented (anthers 0 09 cm long, filaments 0 2 cm long), connective rather strongly overhanging

Pistillate flower pedicel 1 1 cm long, tepals five, ovate to obovate, sometimes with involute margins, 0 5 - 0 6 cm long, 0 3 - 0 5 cm broad, styles three, two-lobed, stigmatic surface covers all sides of the capitate stigmatic lobes, stigmatic papillae in the form of capitate glandular hairs, ovary three-celled, 0 5 cm long, 0 27 cm broad, wings three, very unequal, the largest one ca 0.48 cm broad, the other two ca 0 05 - 0 08 cm broad; placentae non-divided, very narrow, linear

(Note In the course of this study, it was found that the examined specimen of *Begonia boisiana* differed from the existing descriptions of the section <u>Petermannia</u> These descrepancies were noted as follows

<u>Petermannia</u>	*Begonia boisiana*
1 Staminate tepals two	1 Staminate tepals four
2 Filaments arising on a conoidal column	2 Column none
3. Anthers and filaments approximately of the same length	3. Relative length of anthers and filaments is very different
4. Stigmatic papillae form form helical bands.	4. Stigmatic surface covers all sides of capitate end of stigmatic lobe.
5. Placentae two-parted	5. Placentae undivided
6. Fruit wings subequal.	6 Fruit wings very unequal

<u>Section PRITZELIA (Klotzsch) A.DC ,</u>
<u>Ann Sci. Nat. Bot 4,11 137 1859.</u>

Staminate flower tepals four, filaments free, anthers oblong, obtuse, longer than the filaments, connective scarcely overhanging the anther lobes

Pistillate flower tepals five, styles three, very little united below, two-divided in the upper part, persistent, style branches in most cases rather long, on all sides covered with stigmatic surface, placentae non-divided (but according to Irmscher 1925, divided and non-divided placentae can be found within the same ovary), fruit three-celled, mostly with three subequal wings

Climbing herbs or semi-shrubs, mostly glabrous; leaves often very unsymmetrical palmate-pinnately veined or peltate, often purple-red on the under side, bracts and stipules often large; inflorescence not particularly large and expanded, cystoliths (according to Fellerer [7]) present

Typical species· *Begonia dietrichiana* Irmscher and *B tomentosa* Schott *in* Sprengel

Species examined. *Begonia acida* Vellozo, *B. epipsila* Brade, *B. echinosepala* Regel, and *B vitifolia* Schott *in* Sprengel

Begonia acida Vellozo, Fl Flum
10.T 50 1827 Plate XIII.

Herbaceous plant, erect, hairy and covered with coarse scales, stem ca 8 cm tall, leaves almost rounded-cordate, peltate, underneath pilose, inaequilateral, petioles medium-sized, hairy, inflorescence longer than the leaves, terminal, cymous, compound, loose, many-flowered.

Staminate flower pedicel 0.8 cm long, tepals four, at right angles with each other, external tepals orbicular, slightly cordate at the base, 0 83 - 0.85 cm long, 0.83 - 0 84 cm broad, internal tepals irregularly oblong-lanceolate, repand along the margin, 0 63 - 0 66 cm long, 0 30 - 0.33 cm broad; androecium 0.4 cm long, 0.4 cm broad, stamens 0.25 - 0.30 cm long, filaments 0 02 - 0 05 cm long, anthers 0.24 - 0.25 cm long, connective broad, obtuse, moderately overhanging

Pistillate flower: pedicel 0 7 cm long, with one bracteole at the base, tepals five, oblong-elliptic or oblong-obovate, 0.3 - 0 5 cm long, 0.15 - 0.30 cm broad, styles three, twice divided, branches ca. 0.13 cm long; stigmatic surface in the form of helical bands with two or three turns, stigmatic papillae of a tubercle or nipple-like type, ovary three-celled, 0.5 cm long, 0.2 cm broad, wings three, strongly unequal, one large, 0 66 cm broad, the two others vestigial; placentae non-divided, narrow cordate in outline

Begonia echinosepala Regel, Act Hort
Petrop 1 91 1871. Plate XIV.

Branched shrub, stems and branches subglabrous, covered with small wart-like outgrowths, with swollen nodes; stipules ovate-lanceolate, acuminate, scarious, almost of the same length as the petioles, petioles hairy 0.5 - 0.8 cm long, leaves pinnately veined, obliquely cordate, oblong or elliptic-oblong, completely glabrous above, more or less purple-red and becoming glabrous

PLATE XIII. *Begonia acida* Vellozo (Section PRITZELIA A DC)

Fig. 1 Staminate flower
a - general outer view x 1 5
b - portion of the pedicel showing trichomes x 7 5.

Fig. 2 Perianth of the staminate flower x 3

Fig 3 Tepals of the staminate flower
a - outer x 3
b - inner x 3.

Fig 4 Androecium x 5.

Fig 5 Idem, longitudinal section x 5

Fig. 6 Stamens. x 15.

Fig 7 Pistillate flower x 2

Fig 8 Perianth of the pistillate flower. x 4

Fig. 9 Tepals of the pistillate flower x 8.

Fig. 10 General view of the stigmas x 5.

Fig. 11 A pair of stigmatic branches. x 10

Fig. 12 Stigmatic surface. x 60.

Fig 13 Ovary x 5

Fig. 14 Idem, median cross section x 15

PLATE XIII

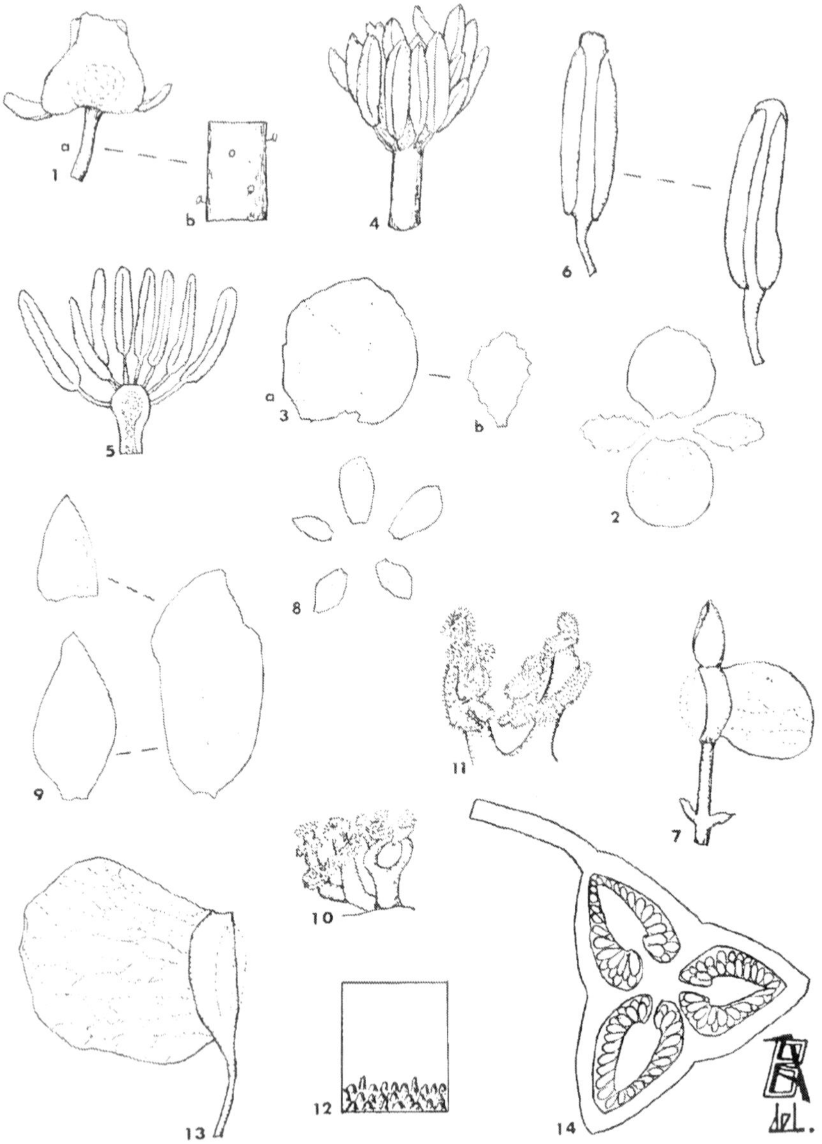

PLATE XIV *Begonia echinosepala* Regel (Section PRITZELIA A.DC.)

Fig 1 Staminate flower
a - general outer view x 3
b - cilia on the abaxial surface of a tepal. x ca 10

Fig 2 Perianth of the staminate flower (adaxial surface) x 3

Fig 3 Tepals of the staminate flower
a - outer (abaxial surface) x 3.
b - inner x 3.

Fig. 4. Androecium x 7

Fig 5. Idem, longitudinal section. x 7

Fig 6. Stamens x 10

Fig 7. Pistillate flower
a - general outer view. x 2
b - portion of the pedicel showing trichomes x 10

Fig. 8 Perianth of the pistillate flower x 5

Fig. 9 General view of the stigmas x 10

Fig. 10. Stigmatic surface x 60

Fig. 11 Ovary x 7 5.

Fig 12. Idem, median cross section
a - general view. x 15
b - one locule showing placenta and ovules x ca 20

PLATE XIV

PLATE XV. *Begonia epipsila* Brade (Section PRITZELIA A DC)

Fig 1 Staminate flower
a - general outer view x 3
b - portion of the pedicel x 10

Fig 2 Perianth of the staminate flower x 3

Fig 3 Tepals of the staminate flower
a - outer. x 3.
b - inner x 3

Fig 4 Androecium x 9 5

Fig. 5. Idem, longitudinal section x 10

Fig 6 Stamens x 15.

Fig. 7 Pistillate flower x 1 5.

Fig. 8. Perianth of the pistillate flower. x 2

Fig 9 One of the tepals of the pistillate flower x 7 5.

Fig 10 General view of the stigmas. x ca 7 5

Fig 11 A pair of stigmatic branches.
a - front view. x 15.
b - side view x 15

Fig 12 Stigmatic surface x 60.

Fig. 13 Ovary. x 5.

Fig. 14. Idem, median cross section x 10

PLATE XV

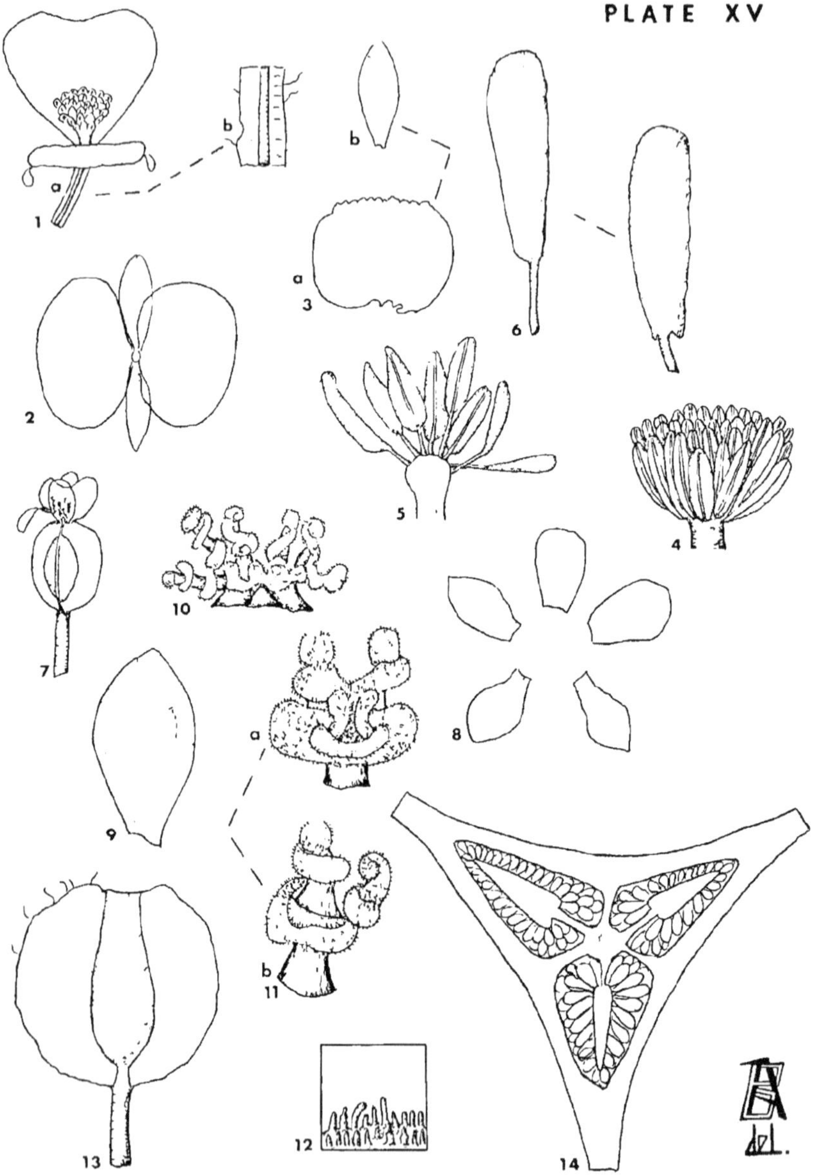

underneath, ca. 6 cm long, 2 5 cm broad, irregularly serrulate along the margin, inflorescence many-flowered, axillary, shaped like an umbel, shorter than the leaves, with glabrous or loosely pilose branches, flowers white

Staminate flower pedicel 0.66 cm long, tepals four, cross-wise oppositely arranged, external tepals broadly cordate-orbiculate, 0.90 - 0 93 cm long, 1.00 - 1 03 cm broad, with a tuft of cilia in the center of the abaxial surface, internal tepals irregularly obovate, repand along the margin, on both sides smooth and glabrous, 0.5 - 0 33 cm long, 0 20 - 0 30 cm broad, androecium 0.4 cm long, 0 4 cm broad, stamens 0 31 - 0 34 cm long, anthers 0 24 - 0 25 cm long, filaments 0 06 - 0 10 cm long, connective broad, obtuse, overhanging

Pistillate flower pedicel 0 4 cm long, tepals five, cordate to oblong, sometimes with involute margins, 0 30 - 0 56 cm long, 0 15 - 0.45 cm broad, styles three, two-divided, branches 0 11 cm long, stigmatic surface forms helical bands with one to two turns, stigmatic papillae of a wart-like or nipple-like type, ovary three-celled, 0 7 cm long, 0.2 cm broad, wings three, subequal, 0 22 - 0 23 cm broad, placentae non-divided, narrowly or irregularly ovate in outline

Begonia epipsila Brade, Arquiv.Jard Bot
Rio de Janeiro **8**:227, t.1 1948. Plate XV

Semi-shrub 30 - 50 cm tall, stems erect, branched, downy; leaves obliquely ovate, shortly acuminate, cordate at the base, entire, sometimes indistinctly angulate, 7 - 10 cm long, 3 - 5 cm broad, green, completely glabrous above, red and densely downy with rust-colored hairs underneath and on the margins, petioles red, 2 5 - 8 cm long, rusty downy, stipules membranous, ovate, 0.12 - 0 24 cm long, 0 10 - 0.15 cm broad, on the outer side hairy, persistent, inflorescence many-flowered, axillary, dichasial, a little longer than the leaves, producing both kinds of flowers; flowers whitish.

Staminate flower pedicel 0 5 cm long; tepals four, at right angles with each other, external tepals broad, transversely elliptic, slightly cordate at the base, 0 60 - 0.63 cm long, 0.9 - 0.93 cm broad, internal tepals narrow obovate or narrow elliptic-obovate, 0 56 - 0 60 cm long, 0 16 - 0 23 cm broad, androecium 0 35 cm long, 0 35 cm broad, stamens 0 4 cm long, anthers 0 25 cm long, filaments 0.15 cm long.

Pistillate flower pedicel 0 75 cm long, tepals five, obovate, oblong-obovate or elliptic, obovate, 0 75 - 0.80 cm long, 0.40 - 0.60 cm broad, styles three, twice divided, branches ca 0 16 cm long, stigmatic surface forms helical bands with two to three turns, stigmatic papillae of a rod-like type, ovary three-celled, 1.05 cm long, 0 4 cm broad, wings three, unequal, downy with minute soft hairs, placentae non-divided, very narrowly cordate in outline

Begonia vitifolia Schott *in* Sprengel, Syst. 4.
Cur Post 407 1827 Plate XVI

Stem at length glabrate, leaves transversely ovate or rounded-kidney-shaped, palmately-6-7-veined, angular-lobate, serrulate, covered with short stellate hairs, sparsely above and more densely underneath, stipules ovate-oblong, acute, glabrous, inflorescence axillary, longer than the leaves, dichasial, many-flowered, producing both kinds of flowers

Staminate flower pedicel 0.75 cm long, tepals four, cross-wise oppositely arranged, external tepals ovate, slightly cordate at the base, 1.0 - 1 1 cm long, 0 60 - 0 66 cm broad, with a cavity on the adaxial surface of each tepal, these cavities probably enclose the androecium when the flower is in the bud stage, internal tepals oblong or oblong-lanceolate, 0 80 - 0 83 cm long, 0.26 - 0 30 cm broad, androecium 0 54 cm long, 0 88 cm broad, stamens of two kinds, the outer or short-filamented (anthers 0 26 cm long, filaments 0.10 cm long) and inner or long-filamented (anthers 0 26 cm long, filaments 0.15 cm long), connective obtuse or acute, more or less overhanging

Pistillate flower pedicel 0.5 cm long, tepals five, ovate or oblong-ovate, sometimes acuminate, 0 6 - 0.7 cm long, 0 25 - 0.30 cm broad, styles three, two-divided, on all sides covered with stigmatic surface, stigmatic papillae of a wart-like or tubercle-like type; ovary three-celled, 0 6 cm long, 0.25 cm broad, wings three very unequal, the largest one 0 83 cm broad, the other two almost vestigial, placentae non-divided, cordate in outline

Section REICHENHEIMIA (Klotzsch) A DC ,
Prodromus 15,1·385 1864.

Staminate flower tepals four, seldom two, but in the latter case the stem is erect, filaments free or united below, anthers obovate or oblong, of equal length with the filaments, connective not overhanging.

Pistillate flower· tepals two to six, styles three, mostly persistent, united below, shortly two-divided in the upper part, stigmatic papillae form a continuous helical band with one turn, placentae undivided, fruits three-celled, with three small unequal wings.

Mostly stemless or almost stemless herbs with tuberous or thick rhizome, basilar inflorescence and palmately veined, somewhat lobed or peltate leaves; stipules persistent.

Type species *Begonia tenera* Koenig *in* Dryander

Species examined *Begonia floccifera* Beddome, *B goegoensis* N.E Brown, and *B sudjanae* Jannson.

PLATE XVI. *Begonia vitifolia* Schott *in* Sprengel (Section PRITZELIA A DC)

Fig 1 Staminate flower, general outer view x 2

Fig 2 Perianth of the staminate flower x 3

Fig. 3 Tepals of the staminate flower
a - outer (showing cavity on its surface) x 4
b - inner. x 4

Fig 4 Androecium x 5

Fig 5 Stamens
a - short-filamented. x 10
b - long-filamented x 10

Fig 6 Pistillate flower, general outer view x 3.

Fig 7 Perianth of the pistillate flower x 5

Fig 8 General view of the stigmas x 10

Fig. 9. Stigmatic surface. x 60

Fig 10 Ovary x 4

Fig. 11. Idem, median cross section. x 12

PLATE XVI

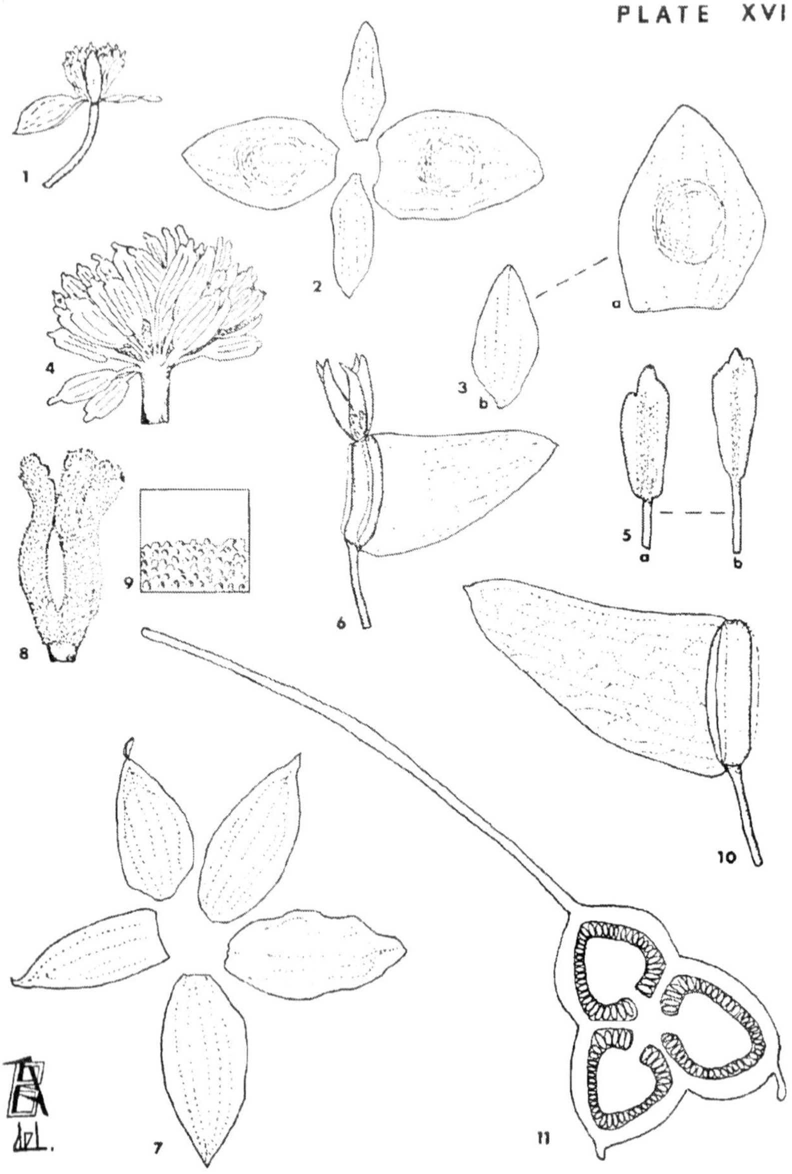

PLATE XVII *Begonia floccifera* Beddome (Section REICHENHEIMIA A.DC)

Fig 1 Staminate flower x 3.

Fig 2 Perianth of the staminate flower
a - two-tepal type of the perianth x 5
b - four-tepal type of the perianth x 5.

Fig 3 Tepals of the staminate flower
a - outer. x 3.
b - inner. x 3

Fig. 4. Androecium x 7

Fig 5. Idem, longitudinal section x 10.

Fig 6 Stamens x 20

Fig. 7 Pistillate flower x 3

Fig 8 Perianth of the pistillate flower x 5

Fig 9 Tepals of the pistillate flower x 10.

Fig. 10 General view of the stigmas x 10.

Fig 11 Stigmatic surface x 60

Fig 12. Ovary x 5

Fig 13. Idem, median cross section
a - general view. x 15
b - one locule showing placenta and ovules x ca 30.

PLATE XVII

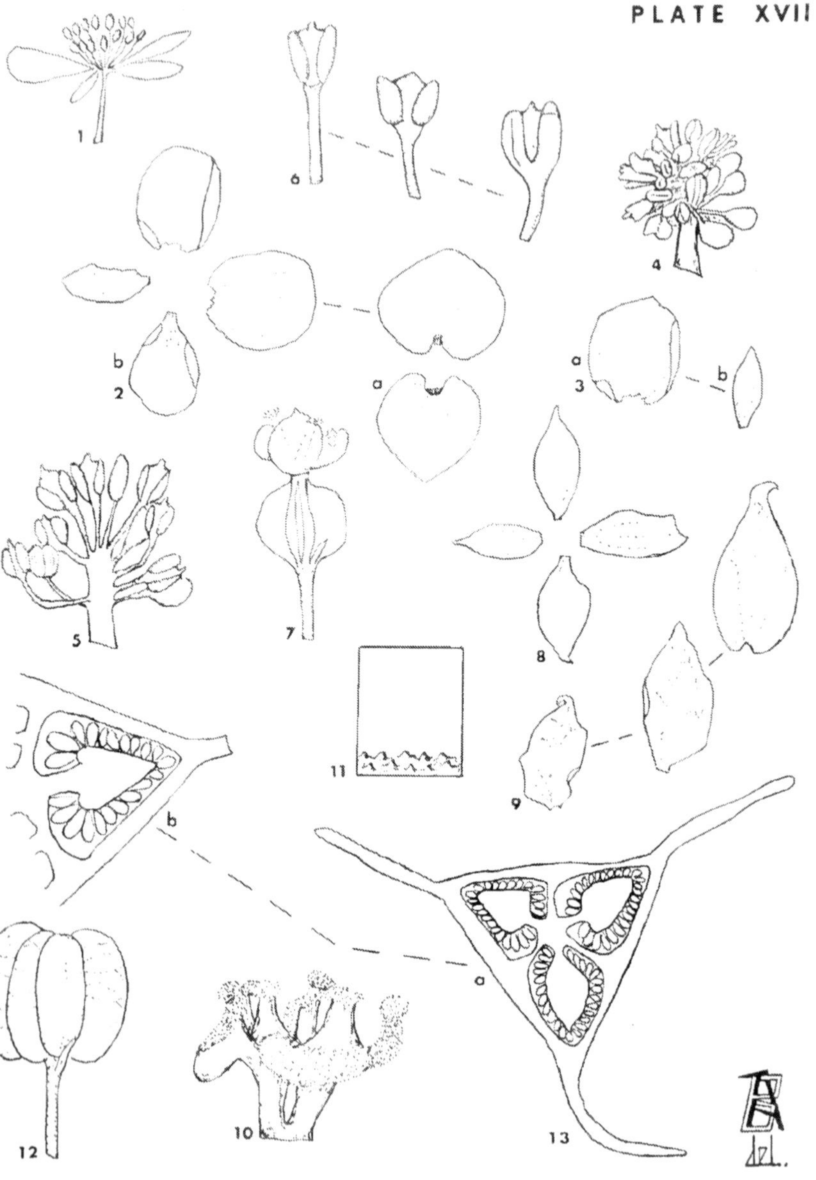

PLATE XVIII. *Begonia goegoensis* N E. Brown (Section REICHENHEIMIA A DC)

Fig 1 Staminate flower, general outer view x 1 5

Fig 2 Perianth of the staminate flower x 3

Fig 3 Tepals of the staminate flower.
a - outer x 3
b - inner x 3.

Fig 4. Androecium. x 10.

Fig 5 Stamens
a - front view x ca 15
b - side view x ca.15

Fig 6 Pistillate flower, general outer view x 2

Fig 7 Perianth of the pistillate flower (abaxial surface) x 2

Fig 8 A pair of stigmatic branches x 10.

Fig 9 Stigmatic surface x 60.

Fig 10 Ovary x 5

Fig 11 Idem, median cross section x 8.

PLATE XVIII

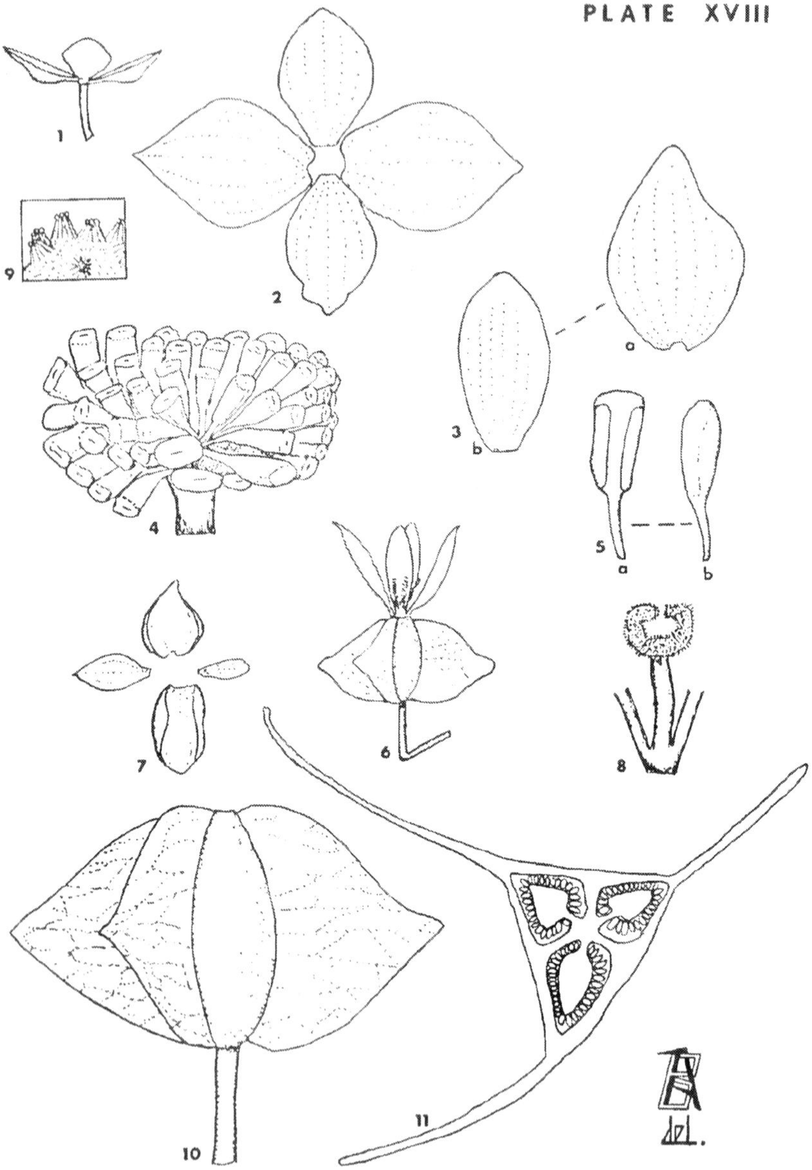

Begonia floccifera Beddome,
Ic Pl Ind Or 1 23 1864 Plate XVII

Stemless, at the apex of the rhizome furnished with large scarious bracts, young leaves densely woolly on both sides, at length subglabrous above, obliquely semicordate to suborbicular, not peltate, irregularly dentate or repand along the margin, generally broader than long, petioles very woolly, inflorescence basilar (arising from the rhizome), many-flowered, dichasial, compound, producing both kinds of flowers

Staminate flower· pedicel 0 4 cm long, tepals two or four, in the latter case they are at right angles with each other, external tepals cordate-orbiculate to obovate, 0.58 - 0 60 cm long, 0.40 - 0 46 cm broad, internal tepals oblong, 0.4 cm long, 0 14 cm broad, androecium 0 42 cm long, 0 35 cm broad, stamens 0 12 - 0.15 cm long, anthers 0 060 - 0 075 cm long, filaments 0 060 - 0 095 cm long, connective acute or obtuse, overhanging a little

Pistillate flower, pedicel 0 5 cm long, tepals four, cross-wise oppositely arranged, elliptic- or oblong-lanceolate, 0 5 - 0 6 cm long, 0.2 - 0 3 cm broad, styles three, two-divided, with broad and thick processes or swellings at the base of the stigmatic branches, branches ca. 0 18 cm long, stigmatic surface forms helical bands with one or two turns, stigmatic papillae of a conelet- or wart-like type, ovary three-celled, 0 5 cm long, 0.2 cm broad, wings three, subequal, 0.17 - 0 20 cm broad, placentae non-divided, ovate in outline

Begonia goegoensis N E Brown,
Gard Chron. 2 71. 1882. Plate XVIII.

Stem short, creeping, rooting, green, with small white blotches, internodes almost undeveloped, very short, stipules broadly ovate, acute, awned, reddish tinted, ca. 0 10 - 0 14 cm long, ca. 0.08 - 0 12 cm broad, petioles ca 7 6 - 11 3 cm long, 0 05 - 0.08 cm thick, four-angled, glabrous, leaves peltate, 6-7-veined, orbicular-ovate, shortly cuspidate-acuminate, ca 11.3-17.9 cm long, 7 78 - 15.24 cm broad, subglabrous, bullate, subrevolute-crenate and very sparsely ciliate along the margin, dark green above, purple-red underneath, inflorescence cymose, repeatedly forked, ebracteate or with very few minute, subulate bracts.

Staminate flower pedicels 0 8 cm long, tepals four, at right angles with each other, external tepals obovate-cordate, acuminate, 1 1 - 1 2 cm long, 0 8 - 0 9 cm broad, internal tepals obovate or oblong-obovate, 0 7 - 0.9 cm long, 0.53 - 0.60 cm broad, androecium 0 3 cm long, 0.5 cm broad, stamens 0 21 - 0.22 cm long, anthers ca. 0.12 - 0 13 cm long, filaments ca 0 08 - 0.09 cm long, connective broad, obtuse, overhanging a little.

Pistillate flower pedicel 1 0 cm long, tepals four, cordate, elliptic or oblong, sometimes acuminate and occasionally with the margins involute, 0.5 - 0.8 cm long, 0.2 - 0 6 cm broad; styles three, twice divided, stigmatic branches curved, forming a crescent-shaped structure, on all sides covered with stigmatic surface, stigmatic papillae dense, forming conical, pyramid-like piles, ovary three-celled, 0 8 cm long, 0 37 cm broad, wings three, unequal, the largest one 0 7 cm broad, the other two 0 41 - 0 57 cm broad, placentae undivided, broadly or narrowly ovate in outline

Begonia sudjanae Jansson,
Acta Hort Gotoburg **26** 1 1963 Plate XIX

Rhizome short, thick, creeping on the ground surface, leaves asymmetrical, peltate, broadly ovate to suborbiculate, wrinkled, covered with bristles, evenly, over the whole surface above, mostly along the veins underneath, 14 - 18 cm long, 9 - 12 cm broad, petioles 10 - 18 cm long, densely covered with whitish, curly hairs, stipules triangulate-ovate, 0 6 - 1 0 cm long, 0.5 - 0.7 cm broad, on the outer side and along the margin beset with long hairs; inflorescence dichasial, branches repeatedly forked three or four times, bracts lanceolate, pilose, 0 3 - 0.5 cm long, 0.1 - 0.2 cm broad

Staminate flower pedicel 0 6 cm long, tepals three, external tepals elliptic-oblong, on the apex retuse, 0 58 - 0 60 cm long, 0 46 - 0 48 cm broad, internal tepals lanceolate, 0 6 cm long, 0 3 cm broad, androecium 0.34 cm long, 0 26 cm broad, stamens 0 09 - 0 10 cm long, anthers 0.05 - 0.06 cm long, filaments 0 03 - 0 05 cm long, connective not overhanging.

Pistillate flower. pedicel 0 8 cm long, tepals two, broadly cordate or orbiculate, 0 75 - 0 80 cm long, 0.90 - 1 00 cm broad; styles three, twice divided, branches ca 0.8 cm long, stigmatic surface forms helical bands with one turn, stigmatic papillae nipple-like and pinnacle-like, ovary three celled, 0.5 cm long, 0.2 cm broad, wings three, unequal, 0.3 - 0 5 cm broad, placentae undivided, ovate in outline

(Note: In the existing descriptions of *B. sudjanae*, staminate flowers are described as having four tepals and pistillate flowers as having three tepals, however, the flowers examined for this study, had three tepals in the staminate flowers and two tepals in the pistillate flowers.)

Section TETRACHIA Brade,
Rodriguesia **18**·21. 1945.

Staminate flower tepals two, stamens affixed to an almost flat torus, anthers oblong, shorter than the filaments

Pistillate flower. tepals six, subequal; styles four, scarcely united below, divided above, branches more often are twisted, stigmatic papillae form continuous helical bands, ovary four-celled, placentae twice-divided, bearing ovules on all sides, fruit four-winged

PLATE XIX *Begonia sudjanae* Jannson (Section REICHENHEIMIA A DC)

Fig. 1. Staminate flower x 3

Fig 2 Perianth of the staminate flower x 3

Fig. 3 Tepals of the staminate flower
a - outer x 5
b - inner. x 5

Fig. 4 Androecium. x 10

Fig 5 Idem, longitudinal section x 10

Fig. 6 Stamens x 20.

Fig 7 Pistillate flower x 2

Fig. 8 Perianth of the pistillate flower x 3

Fig 9. A pair of stigmatic branches x 10

Fig 10 Stigmatic surface x 60.

Fig 11. Ovary x 6

Fig. 12 Idem, median cross section x 9

PLATE XIX

PLATE XX *Begonia egregia* N E Brown (Section TETRACHIA Brade)

Fig. 1 Staminate flower, general outer view x 3

Fig 2. Perianth of the staminate flower x 3.

Fig. 3 Androecium x 8

Fig. 4 Stamens x 15

Fig. 5. Pistillate flower, general outer view x 2

Fig. 6. Perianth of the pistillate flower. x 3.

Fig 7. General view of the stigmas. x 5

Fig. 8 A pair of stigmatic branches x 10

Fig 9. Stigmatic surface x 60

Fig. 10. Ovary x 4

Fig 11 Idem, median cross section x 11

PLATE XX

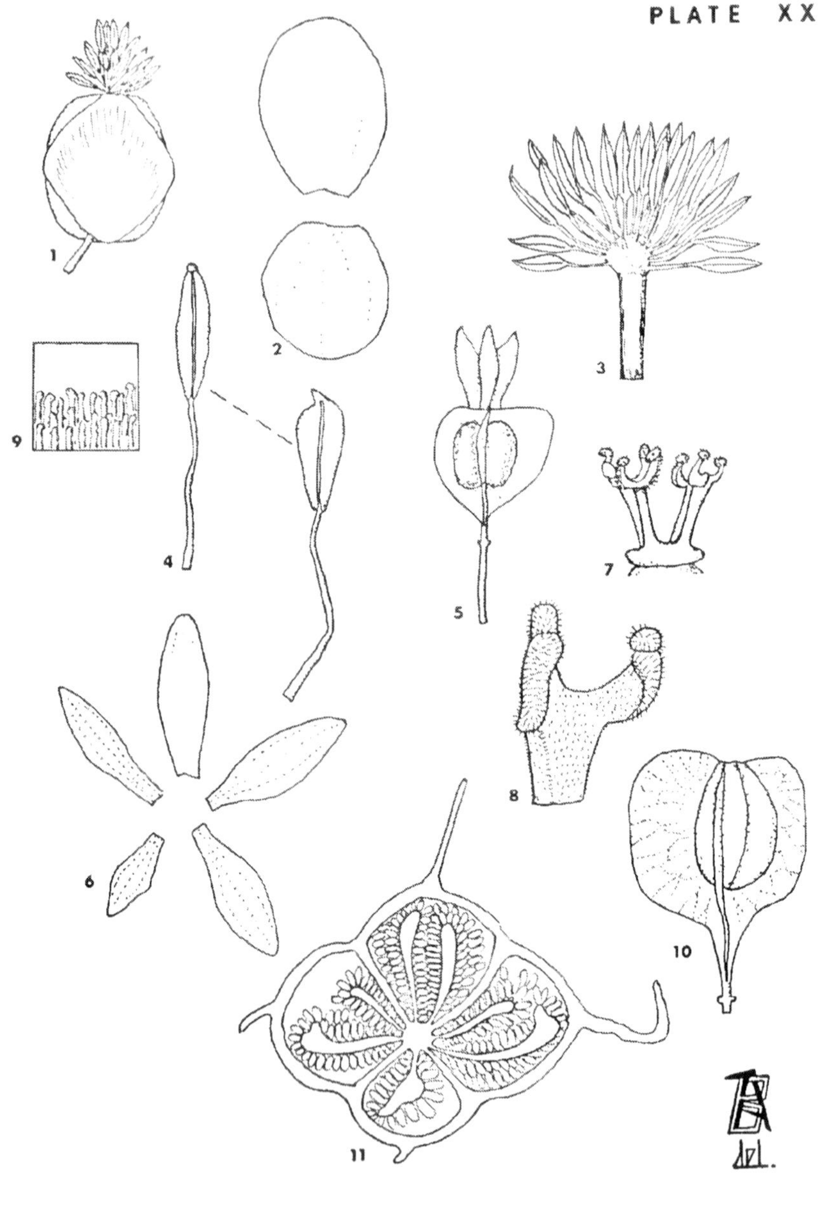

Shrubs, leaves more often peltate, pinnately veined or almost palmate-pinnately veined

Type species *Begonia quadrilocularis* Brade

Species examined *Begonia egregia* N E. Brown.

Begonia egregia N.E. Brown,
Gard Chron. 1·346 1887 Plate XX

Semi-shrub 90 - 120 cm tall, young shoots herbaceous, fleshy, covered with thin, brownish tomentum, leaves peltate, 20 3 - 27.9 cm long, 5 20 - 10.16 cm broad, obliquely oblong, acuminate at the apex, unsymmetrical at the base, bright green, rough with papillae above, pale green, soft hairy underneath, petioles 5 20- 7 62 cm long, sparsely tomentose at the base, short haired in the upper part, stipules caducous, 0 19 cm long, lanceolate, acute, tomentose on the surface and ciliate along the margin, inflorescence drooping, many-flowered, cymous, with sparsely pubescent peduncle and branches

Staminate flower pedicel 0 25 cm long, tepals two, orbiculate-obovate, 0.80 - 0 95 cm long, 0.80 - 0 83 cm broad, androecium 0 34 cm long, 0 56 cm broad, stamens ca 0.38 cm long, anthers 0.16 - 0 17 cm long, filaments 0 21 - 0 22 cm long, connective overhanging a little.

Pistillate flower pedicel 0 95 cm long, tepals five, oblong-lanceolate, 0.60 - 0 75 cm long, 0 20 - 0 30 cm broad, styles four, two divided, each pair of branches forms a crescent-shaped structure with capitate ends, stigmatic surface forms helical bands, stigmatic papillae of a mixed type, rods plus capitate hairs, ovary four-celled, 1 0 cm long, 0 4 cm broad, wings four, very unequal, the two largest 0.19 - 0.20 cm broad, of the other two, one is ca. 0.07 cm broad and one is almost vestigial; placentae partly not divided, partly two divided into variously shaped, narrow lobes

Section TETRAPHILA (A DC.) A. Baranov *emend.*
A Baranov, Phytologia **24** 155. 1972.

Staminate flower. tepals four, stamens heaped into an egg-shaped, sessile, conical cluster, anthers oblong, sessile.

Pistillate flower: tepals four, of these the two inner ones are more narrow; styles four, three or even two, united below, linear, towards apex gradually widening (but not capitate), on the inner surface, near the apex, provided with a band of stigmatic papillae; ovary elongate, fusiform-cylindrical, four-celled, wingless

Epiphytic and climbing, often richly branches herbs, glabrous or covered with stellate hairs; stem nodes sometimes producing roots, leaves pinnately veined; inflorescence lateral, axillary, cymose, in most cases few-flowered, short, stipules large, deciduous

Type species: *Begonia mannii* Hooker *f*.

Species examined *Begonia mannii* Hooker *f*.

Begonia mannii Hooker *f*
Bot. Mag. **90** t 5434 1864 Plate XXI.

Epiphytic; stem erect, fleshy, ca 45 75 - 61.00 cm tall, glabrous, leaves 10.0 - 12.5 cm long, petiolate, ovate-oblong, acuminate, cordate at the base and asymmetrical a little, distantly and irregularly subdentate, pinnately veined, glabrous above, punctulate-squamulose, and rufous-hairy along the veins underneath, petioles 2 5 - 5 0 cm long, rufous-hairy, stipules large, lanceolate, acuminate, ca. 1.8 cm long, deciduous, male and female inflorescences separate, axillary, shorter than the leaves, dichasial, few-flowered

Staminate flower pedicel ca. 0.8 cm long, tepals four cross-wise oppositely arranged, external tepals ovate-cordate, with involute margins, 0 90 - 0.93 cm long, 0.7 - 0 8 cm broad, internal tepals oblong-lanceolate or narrowly obovate, 0 9 - 1.0 cm long, 0.36 - 0 37 cm broad, androecium 0 45 cm long, 0.30 cm broad, stamens sessile, 0 40 - 0 41 cm long, connective acutish, overhanging a little

Pistillate flower pedicel 1 5 cm long, tepals five, elliptic to narrowly obovate, 1 3 - 1 6 cm long, 0.4 - 0 9 cm broad, styles four, undivided, shortly united below, stigmatic surface in the form of linear bands on the undersurface of the apical, dilated portion of the styles, stigmatic papillae of a pinnacle-like type, ovary four-celled, 1.9 cm long, ca. 0 3 cm broad, cylindrical-fusiform, wingless, densely covered with stellate hairs, placentae variously-shaped, undivided.

(Note: Although in the classical diagnosis of the section the ovary is described as four-celled, in *Begonia mannii* the number of cells varies from three to five.)

Section TRACHELOCARPUS A.DC ,
Martius' Fl Bras Begon. p. 381 1861.

Staminate flower· tepals two, filaments completely united into a slender column; anthers obovate, sessile on the column's apex.

Pistillate flower tepals three, styles three, united below, each with two horn-like branches, stigmatic papillae form helical bands with one twist, placentae not divided, ovary and fruit crowned with a more or less long, slender beak or neck, fruit three-celled, with three narrow, dentate wings.

Creeping herbs; leaves different from the usual begonia leaf-type, they are oblong to lanceolate, glabrous, pinnately veined, stipules persistent;

PLATE XXI *Begonia mannii* Hook f (Section TETRAPHILA (A DC) A Baranov *emend*)

Fig 1 Staminate flower
a - general outer view x 1 5
b - portion of the pedicel showing trichomes. x 8.

Fig 2 Perianth of the staminate flower x 3

Fig 3 Tepals of the staminate flower
a - outer x 3
b - inner x 3.

Fig 4 Androecium x 8

Fig 5 Idem, longitudinal section x 10

Fig 6. Stamens x 10.

Fig 7 Pistillate flower
a - general outer view x 1.5
b - trichomes on the ovary x ca 8
c - bracteole found on the ovary at the base of the perianth x ca.3

Fig 8. Perianth of the pistillate flower x 1 5

Fig. 9. General view of the stigmas. x 10

Fig 10 Stigmatic surface x 60

Fig. 11. Ovary x 5.

Fig. 12. Idem, median cross section x 10

PLATE XXI

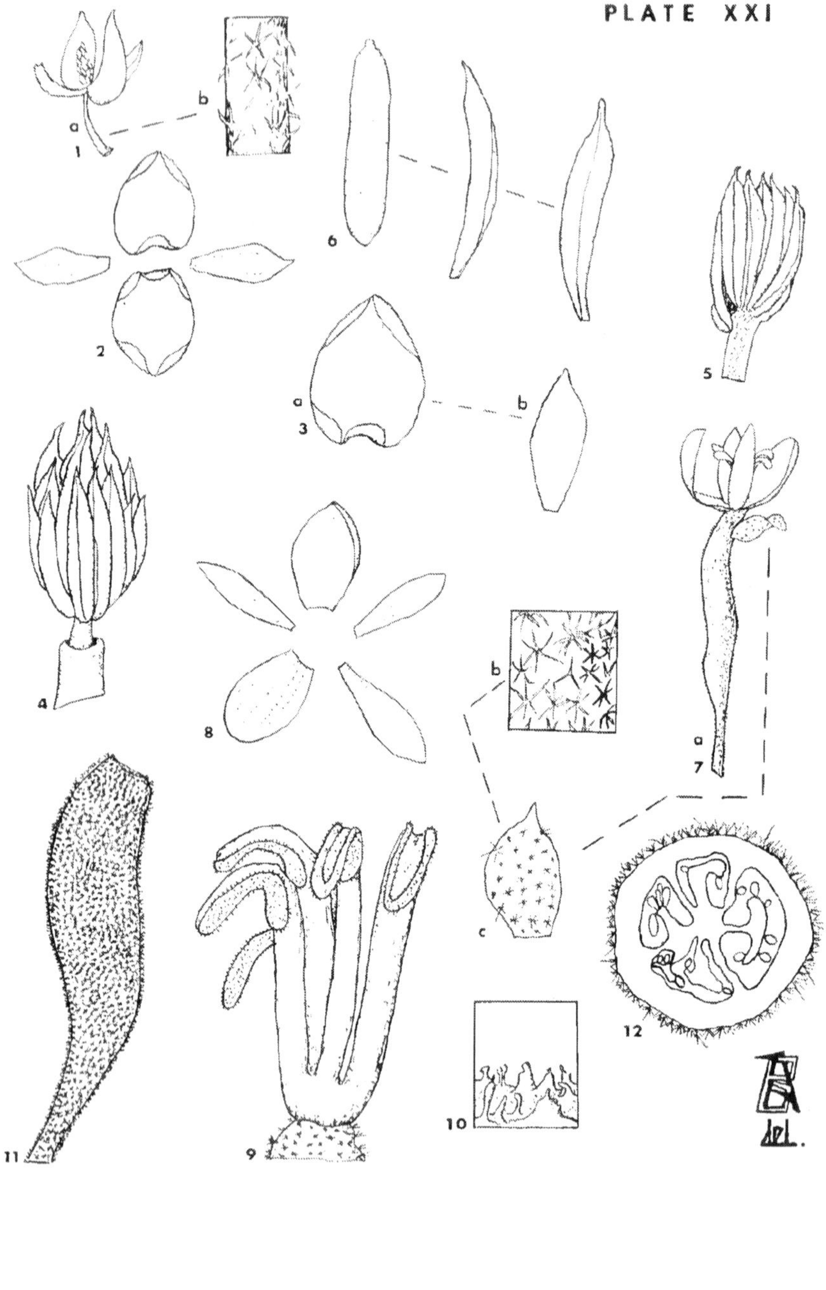

PLATE XXII *Begonia herbacea* Vellozo (Section TRACHELOCARPUS A DC)

Fig 1 Staminate flower, general outer view. x 2.

Fig 2. Perianth of the staminate flower x 3

Fig 3. One of the two tepals of the staminate flower x 3

Fig 4 Androecium. x 7.

Fig 5 Idem, longitudinal section x 10

Fig. 6 Stamens. x 20

Fig. 7 Pistillate flower x 1 5

Fig 8 Perianth of the pistillate flower x 3

Fig 9. General view of the stigmas x 5

Fig 10 A pair of stigmatic branches. x 10

Fig 11 Stigmatic surface x 60

Fig 12 Ovary x 3

Fig. 13 Idem, median cross section x 8

PLATE XXII

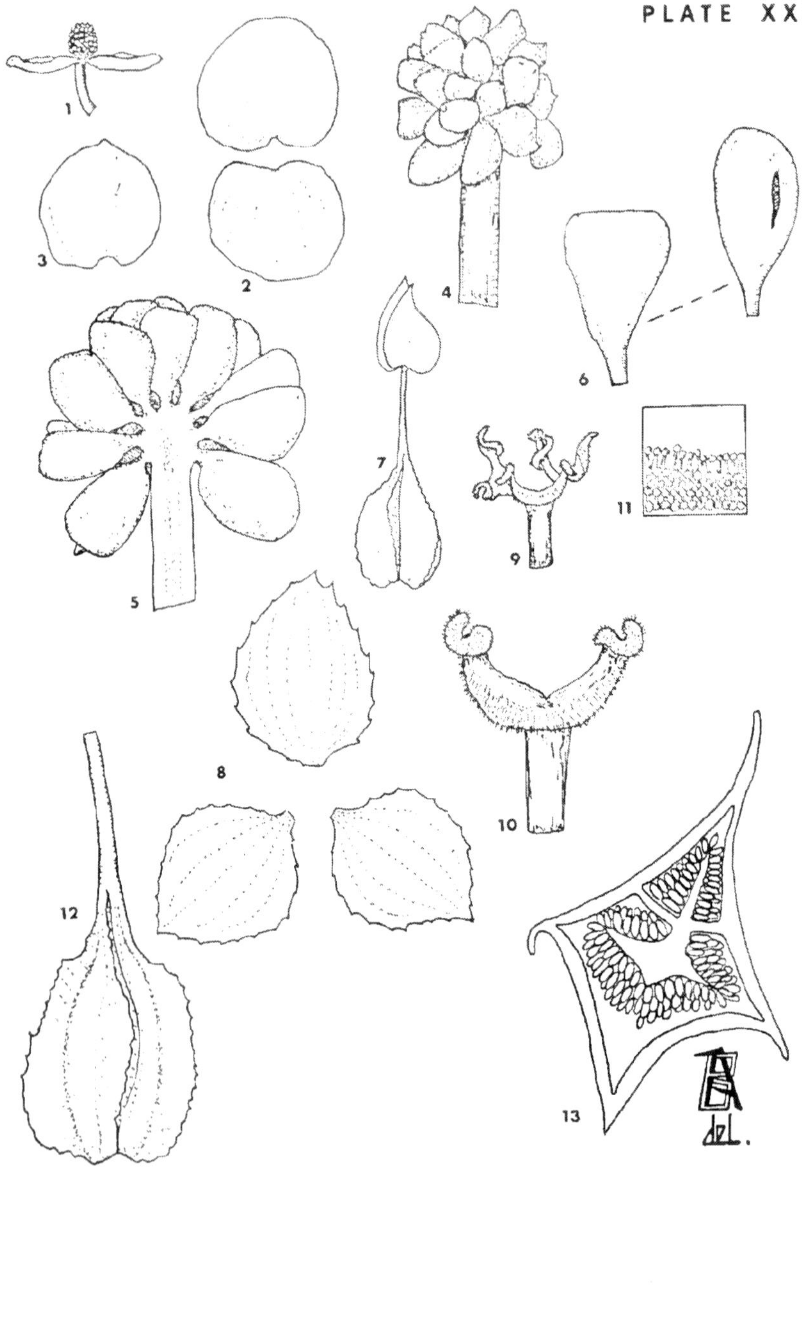

inflorescences basilar, male and female separate, the male, long-peduncled, several flowered, the female, almost sessile, solitary.

Typical species *Begonia herbacea* Vellozo and *B rhizocarpa* Fischer *in* A DC.

Species examined *Begonia herbacea* Vellozo

Begonia herbacea Vellozo,
Fl. Flum 10 t 53 1827 Plate XXII

Stemless, rhizome creeping; leaves radical, oblong-lanceolate, acute, serrate along the margin, stipules ovate, acuminate, inflorescences shorter than the leaves, the male one axillary, erect, with forked branches

Staminate flower pedicel 0 5 cm long; tepals two, orbiculate-cordate, 0 80 - 0.81 cm long, 0.80 - 0.85 cm broad; androecium 0 3 cm long, 0 3 cm broad, stamens subsessile, 0 15 cm long.

Pistillate flower: pedicel none; tepals three, broadly ovate or ovate-orbiculate, repand-serrate along the margin, 1.1 - 1.2 cm long, 0.85 - 0 95 cm broad, styles three, each with two horn-shaped stigmatic branches, ca 0 24 cm long, stigmatic surface forms continuous helical bands with one turn, stigmatic papillae in the form of capitate, glandular hairs, ovary two-celled, sessile, 1 4 cm long, 0.64 cm broad, wings four, narrow, serrate along the margin, unequal, 0.01 - 0.22 cm broad, placentae not divided, cuneiform in outline

(Note According to the existing literature, the ovary in this species is three-celled In the specimen examined for this study, the ovary was (ab-normally?) two-celled, with two placentae in one of the cells.)

Section WEILBACHIA (Klotzsch *et* Oersted)
A DC , Ann.Sci. Nat. Bot 4,11.134 1859

Staminate flower tepals two or four, filaments free, anthers oblong, obtuse, longer than the filaments

Pistillate flower tepals two or three, styles two, not persistent, united below, two-lobed; stigmatic branches short, stigmatic papillae form a continuous helical band, ovary two-celled, triquetrous, placentae twice divided, the undivided placental segments are occasionally lobed, fruit triquetrous, two-celled, drooping, wings three, unequal

Stemless or almost stemless herbs with creeping rhizome and long-petioled, palmately veined leaves

Type species *Begonia reptans* Bentham

Species examined *Begonia pustulata* Liebmann

Begonia pustulata Liebmann,
Kjoeb. Vidensk Meddel 6 1853 Plate XXIII

Stemless, rhizome creeping, rooting, leaves obliquely, broadly ovate, palmately-9-veined, cordate at the base, shortly acuminate at the apex, setose-denticulate along the margin, bullate and setiferous above, foveolate and rough hairy along the veins underneath, petioles long, very densely covered with rough, rufous hairs, stipules elongate-lanceolate, somewhat hairy, inflorescence short, few-flowered, bracts oblong, acuminate, scarcely hairy, deciduous

Staminate flower pedicel 1.4 cm long, tepals four at right angles with each other, external tepals broadly ovate or obovate, acutish on the apex, on the abaxial surface hairy, 1.7 - 1 8 cm long, 1 1 - 1 2 cm broad, internal tepals narrowly obovate or spatulate, on both sides glabrous, 1.3 - 1 4 cm long, 0 2 - 0 4 cm broad, androecium 0.45 cm long, 0 30 cm broad, stamens 0 30 - 0 32 cm long, anthers 0.19 - 0 20 cm long, filaments 0.10 - 0 13 cm long.

Pistillate flower pedicel 0.8 cm long, tepals three, two large, irregularly orbiculate, 1 00 - 1 03 cm long, 0.96 - 1 03 cm broad, on the abaxial surface short hairy, the third tepal small and lanceolate, 0 6 cm long, 0.2 cm broad, on both sides glabrous, styles three, two-divided, branches short, 0 15 - 0 16 cm long, stigmatic surface covers capitate ends of stigmatic brahcnes, stigmatic papillae form conical, pyramid-like piles, ovary two-celled, 0 7 cm long, 0 14 cm broad, wings three, unequal, the largest one 0.49 cm broad, the other two 0.25 - 0 37 cm broad, placentae two-divided with waved lobes

Discussion and Conclusions

The results of this study can be viewed from two different perspectives--morphological and taxonomical. From a morphological point of view, the preceding descriptions of the *Begonia* sections and species demonstrate differences on both the sectional and species level, as well as in the structure of their vegetative and reproductive organs.

In discussing the differences among sections, one must note that these groups of species can differ in a number of ways, e g. the type of stems and leaves, character of inflorescences, flowers or fruits. There are sections which include semi-shrubs and other woody plants (Tetrachia, Barya, Casparya and Gaerdtia), which can also be climbers (Enita) Other sections include herbaceous begonias, stemless (Reichenheimia and Weilbachia) or erect caulescent (Begonia and Doratometra), climbing (Tetraphila) or creeping (Trachelocarpus) plants. Herbaceous species in most cases are perennials, but there is one section (Huszia) whose members are annuals. The leaves can be palmately- (Doratometra), pinnately- (Casparya) or palmately-pinnately-veined (Barya and Begonia), long- (Huszia) or short-petioled (Haagea and Lepsia) Leaves in

PLATE XXIII *Begonia pustulata* Liebmann (Section WEILBACHIA A DC.)

Fig 1 Staminate flower.
a - general outer view x 1 5
b - portion of the pedicel showing trichomes x 10

Fig 2 Perianth of the staminate flower (adaxial surface) x 1 5.

Fig 3 Tepals of the staminate flower
a - outer (adaxial surface) x 3.
b - outer (abaxial surface) x 3
c - inner x 3

Fig 4. Androecium. x 10

Fig. 5. Stamens. x 20

Fig 6. Pistillate flower
a - general outer view. x 1.5
b - portion of the pedicel showing trichomes x 10.

Fig 7 Perianth of the pistillate flower
a - outer tepal's abaxial surface x 3
b - trichomes on the abaxial surface x 20
c - outer tepal's adaxial surface x 3
d - inner tepal. x 3.

Fig. 8. General view of the stigmas. x 13

Fig 9. Stigmatic surface x 60.

Fig. 10 Ovary x 5

Fig. 11 Idem, median cross section x 10.

PLATE XXIII

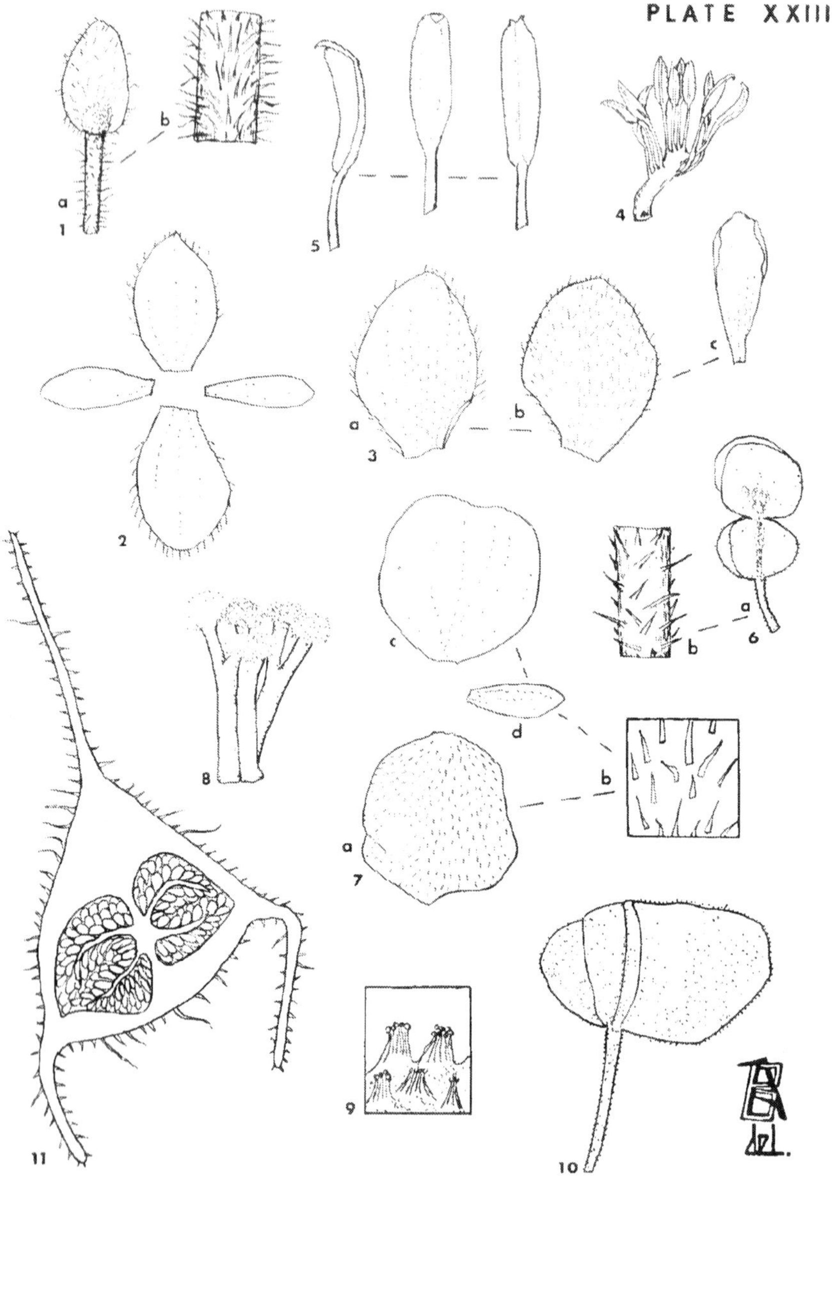

section Trachelocarpus are quite different from the usual begonia leaf-type -- they are oblong, stretched out, and pinnately-veined.

Indumentum (pubescence) is not a sectional character with the exception of one section (Tetraphila) for which stellar pubescence is typical. Presence or absence of cystoliths in the tissues of the *Begonia* plants, however, is a special sectional character. Thus, in section Pritzelia, for example, cystoliths are present, while they are absent in Lepsia, Enita and Begonia. Inflorescence, flower and fruit characters can also differ. In many cases, inflorescences are lateral, axillary (Barya, Doratometra, Enita), arising on vegetative shoots; or they can be basilar, arising on the rhizome, (Reichenheimia and Trachelocarpus), or terminal (Petermannia). In addition, inflorescences can be many-flowered (Enita and Huszia), moderately-flowered (Gaerdtia, Haagea, Pritzelia) or few-flowered (Barya, Doratometra, Lepsia). In the majority of sections under study, inflorescences produce both male and female flowers, but in sections Tetraphila and Trachelocarpus the inflorescences are either purely male or purely female. Furthermore, both inflorescences in Tetraphila have the same morphological structure and approximately the same number of flowers. At the same time, male inflorescence in Trachelocarpus is long-peduncled and few-flowered while female is sessile and one-flowered.

The differences in flower structure occur, first of all, in the number of tepals and then in the type of androecium, stamens and styles. There are, for example, sections with four staminate tepals (Barya, Begonia, Casparya) or with two staminate tepals (Haagea, Petermannia, Tetrachia). The number of pistillate tepals can also differ among various sections. There are, for example, sections with only two (Haagea), three (Trachelocarpus), four (Tetraphila), five (Lepsia, Petermannia, Pritzelia) or six (Tetrachia) pistillate tepals. In other sections the number of tepals varies within certain limits, e.g. two to six (Reichenheimia) four to five (Doratometra), four to six (Barya, Huszia) or five to six (Begonia, Casparya) pistillate tepals.

The stamens can be free (Begonia, Casparya, Gaerdtia, Pritzelia, Weilbachia), united below (Lepsia) or united more or less completely into a column (Barya, Petermannia, Trachelocarpus). The latter group also shows evidence of diversity among sections. In section Trachelocarpus, the filaments are completely united into a column and the anthers are almost sessile on the top of this column. In section Petermannia, the column is rather short and free portions of filaments seem to be rather long. Conversely, in section Barya, the column of stamens is conspicuously extended and the filaments arise on all sides and levels along this column.

The shape of the anthers and their length in relation to filaments may also vary among different sections. Some anthers can be obovate (Gaerdtia, Petermannia, Trachelocarpus) ovate (Barya, Lepsia), oblong (Begonia, Haagea, Pritzelia, Tetrachia, Tetraphila) or linear (Casparya). Conversely, anthers can be approximately equal in length to filaments (Barya, Begonia, Haagea, Petermannia), longer than filaments (Doratometra, Lepsia, Pritzelia, Weilbachia), much shorter than filaments (Enita, Tetrachia) or sessile (Tetraphila,

Trachelocarpus). The degree of protraction of the connective is another section character found in Begonia. The connective can be either overhanging (Begonia, Doratometra, Huszia, Pritzelia) or not overhanging (Haagea, Reichenheimia) the anther lobes

In most sections the number of styles is three, except Weilbachia which has two and Tetrachia and Tetraphila which have four Section Tetraphila differs from all the others in that its styles are not divided

Sections with two-divided styles differ in their structure of branches These can be linear and straight (Barya, Doratometra, Huszia), linear and twisted (Begonia, Lepsia, Tetrachia) or slightly curved and crescent-shaped (Trachelocarpus). Section Casparya whose styles are described as two-divided, with branches divided again several times represents a special case

The arrangement of stigmatic papillae on the styles' branches is still another section character. In most cases, stigmatic papillae form helical bands, in which case the distinction is made on the basis of the number of turns made by the band on a stigmatic branch. Thus there are sections which are characterized by five band turns (Barya) and one or two turns (Doratometra, Gaerdtia) In other sections, stigmatic papillae form either a straight band on the inner sides of stigmatic branches, near their apex (Tetraphila) or cover the branches on all sides (Casparya, Enita, Pritzelia).

As has been mentioned earlier, the structure of stigmatic surfaces of each species under study was carefully examined and it was found that this structure differs significantly among various *Begonia* species As a result of the study, the following five types of stigmatic surfaces have been ascertained

1 Dense, capitate, glandular hairs, e g , in *Begonia* (Doratometra) *franconis* Liebmann and *B* (Lepsia) *foliosa* HBK

2. Capitate, glandular hairs united into conical, pyramid-like piles, e.g. in *Begonia* (Begonia) *schmidtiana* Regel and *B* (Reichenheimia) *goegoensis* N E Brown

3. Pinnacle-like papillae, e g , in *Begonia* (Barya) *boliviensis* A DC and *B.* (Tetraphila) *mannii* Hooker f

4. Rod-like papillae, e g in *Begonia* (Begonia) *pseudolubbersii* Brade and *B* (Tetrachia) *egregia* N.E Brown.

5 Small, low conical, rounded wart-like or nipple-like papillae, e.g in *Begonia* (Enita) *convolvulacea* A.DC and *B* (Pritzelia) *acida* Vellozo

The fifth and last type of stigmatic surfaces comprises the majority of specimens with seven species, while the remaining four groups have four species each These five types are not restricted to any particular section and plants from different sections can be found in the same grouping

In different sections the ovaries are distinguished primarily by the number of cells and by the number and structure of wings In most sections the ovaries are three-celled, but, in the case of Tetrachia and Tetraphila they are four-celled, and in Weilbachia they are two-called

The ovaries usually have three wings (in most sections), but Tetrachia has four, while in two sections, Casparya and Tetraphila, the ovaries are wingless. And, there are still further differences evident between the last two sections, in Casparya, the ovaries are triquetrous, with little horns on the top corners, while in Tetraphila the ovary is fusiform-cylindrical, and without any horns, wings or ribs

Sections with three-winged fruits can be differentiated on the basis of wing characters For example, section Trachelocarpus can be distinguished from other sections by its three very narrow, dentate wings In the other sections the wings are entire on their margins and can be almost equal (Doratometra, Gaerdtia, Haagea, Petermannia) or unequal (Barya, Begonia, Lepsia, Huszia) A group with unequal wings can have further dissimilarities, such as one large and two small wings (Barya), one large wing and two others vestigial or aborted (Huszia), or all three wings being of different size (Begonia, Lepsia)

One special distinctive character in the outer appearance of Trachelocarpus ovary is the presence of a long beak, a feature which was not observed in the members of other sections. Likewise, a special distinctive character of Tetraphila ovary is a dense cover of stellate hairs Furthermore, the fruit of Tetraphila is indehiscent while in other sections it is usually dehiscent

On the basis of placental characters, the sections are divided into two groups, those with two-divided placentae (Barya, Begonia, Casparya) and those with undivided placentae (Doratometra, Enita, Haagea, Lepsia, Pritzelia, Trachelocarpus).

It is a matter of course, then, that the distinctive characters of sections also serve as the distinctive characters for species from different sections. Nevertheless, at the species level, specific differences exist among members of the same section This fact will be demonstrated using section Pritzelia as an example

Four species from section Pritzelia, *Begonia acida* Vellozo, *B epipsila* Brade, *B. echinosepala* Regel and *B. vitifolia* Schott *in* Sprengel have been examined. These four species can be divided, first of all, into two main groups, herbaceous plants (*B. acida*) and woody and semi-woody plants (the remaining three species) Within the woody species category, *B echinosepala* can be easily distinguished from the others by the presence of tufts of cilia on the abaxial surface of external staminate tepals. And, it can also be differentiated from the other two species by its pinnately-veined leaves, almost complete absence of pubescence, and an ovary with three almost equal wings. Of the other two species, *B. epipsila* has stems, petioles, stipules, the undersides of the leaves and the branches of the inflorescence rusty downy, *B. vitifolia* has pubescence of stellate hairs on the young shoots and the leaves on both surfaces are pubescent with stellate hairs. The ovary in these species is provided with very unequal wings, while the leaves are palmately-veined.

The vegetative organs of *Begonia epipsila* and *B. vitifolia* also differ. *B. vitifolia* has leaves transversely ovate or rounded-kidney-shaped, serrulate, 3.75-6.75 cm long, 7.5-10 cm broad, green on both sides, petioles 7.5-12.5 cm long, shortly rough hairy, stipules ovate-oblong, glabrous, 1.6 cm long. *Begonia epipsila* has leaves obliquely ovate, entire, 7-10 cm long, 3-5 cm broad, green and glabrous above, red and rusty-downy underneath, petioles rusty-downy and red, 2.5-8 cm long, stipules ovate, hairy, 0.12-0.24 cm long.

The difference in the structure of stigmatic surfaces between species is equally obvious. On the basis of this character, *Begnoia epipsila* can be assigned to the fourth type, with band-shaped stigmatic surfaces. *Begonia vitifolia* can be classified as the fifth type, with stigmatic surfaces covering style branches entirely, on all sides.

The ovary in *Begonia epipsila* is downy and it is provided with three unequal wings none of which is vestigial. In *Begonia vitifolia* the ovary is glabrous, with three unequal wings, one of the wings is exceptionally large while the other two are almost vestigial.

This study provided a number of descriptions and illustrations of both pistillate and staminate flowers of the *Begonia* species typical of certain sections. This information is quite important because many original descriptions of these species are incomplete owing to the fact that often they have been made on the basis of insufficient material. The associated illustrations are also often lacking. De Candolle, for example, who had described many new species, never illustrated the taxa he had described. Consequently, this study should help fill in some of these gaps.

Unfortunately, in some instances, the study has been restricted by lack of material or by abnormalities found in the flowers of studies species. It appears that wild *Begonia* species under cultivation are likely to produce abnormal flowers. Several examples of such abnormalities have been noted under the descriptions of certain species.

As for the taxonomical and nomenclatural aspects of this paper, the following changes were made: the names of two taxa were corrected and a revised description for one section (Tetraphila) was offered.*

---

*These results appeared in two short papers published elsewhere [1], [2].

It has been noted in the descriptions of several species, that the characters of these species are inconsistent with the characters of the sections to which they belong. A prominent example of such contradictions is *Begonia* (Petermannia) *boisiana* Gagnepain (q v) The following observations are ostensibly relevant to these inconsistencies The current system of classification of *Begonia* species is essentially Klotzcsh's system which was modified and updated by De Candolle and Warburg. Consequently, this system is still at the level of botanical knowledge which existed in the second half of the nineteenth century, when section descriptions and assignment of species to sections were based on superficial morphological similarities or dissimilarities It is obvious then, that the resulting system was far from perfect and that it has been adopted only as a temporary method of classification of the *Begonia* species It is hoped that the advancements in our knowledge of the Begoniaceae will eventually result in a more up-to-date classification system Nevertheless, at the present time, it is more practical to improve the existing system gradually by studying the individual species and sections, rather than attempting to change the entire system and then rewriting the descriptions of all sections.

Returning to the question of evolutionary classification, one could argue that it is still premature to expect such a classification because, as this study has shown, very little is known about the evolutionary morphology and evolutionary patterns of the genus *Begonia*

References Cited

1 Baranov, A. & Barkley, F A. 1972 Some Nomenclatural Changes in the Sections of *Begonia* L Phytologia **24** 155-157.

2 ________ 1973 The Combination *Begonia Fuchsiafolia* Warburg Phytologia **26**.217-220.

3 ________ 1974 The Sections of the Genus *Begonia* Northeastern University Boston 28 pp.

4 Baranov, A 1977 Preliminary Notes on the Structure of Stigmatic Surfaces in the Begoniaceae. Rhodora 79,818:283-287

5. ________. 1979 Flower and Fruit Characters of *Begonia Roxburghii* The Begonian **46** 164-167 & p 173

6. De Candolle, Alphonse 1864 Begoniaceae Prodromus Systematis Naturalis Regni Vegetabilis. 15,1·266-408 & p 417

7. Fellerer, C. 1892 Beitrage z Anatomie u. Systematik d Begoniaceen Univ. Munchen (Ph D. Dissertation).

8 Irmscher, E 1925 Begoniaceae. Engler u. Prantl Die Naturlichen Pflanzenfamilien (Ed. 2) **21**.548-488

9. Warburg, Otto. 1895 Begoniaceae Engler u Prantl. Die Naturlichen Pflanzenfamilien 3 **6a** 121-150

CPSIA information can be obtained
at www.ICGtesting.com
Printed in the USA
LVHW081412281119
638845LV00006B/39/P

9 781341 862601